PENNED WITHOUT INK

Trusting God to Write Your Story

by
SARAH LYNN PHILLIPS

Straight Street Books
Lighthouse Publishing of the Carolinas

PENNED WITHOUT INK BY SARAH LYNN PHILLIPS
Published by Straight Street Books
an imprint of Lighthouse Publishing of the Carolinas
2333 Barton Oaks Dr., Raleigh, NC 27614

ISBN: 978-1-938499-31-9
Copyright © 2016 by Sarah Lynn Phillips
Cover design by Elaina Lee
Interior design by Karthick Srinivasan

Available in print from your local bookstore, online, or from the publisher at:
www.lighthousepublishingofthecarolinas.com.

For more information on this book and the author visit: www.PennedWithoutInk.com.

Brought to you by the creative team at Lighthouse Publishing of the Carolinas:
Eddie Jones, Cindy Sproles, Shonda Savage, Andrea Merrell, and Brian Cross.

Library of Congress Cataloging-in-Publication Data
Phillips, Sarah Lynn
Penned Without Ink / Sarah Lynn Phillips 1st ed.

Printed in the United States of America

You yourselves are our letter, written on our hearts,
known and read by everybody.
You show that you are a letter from Christ,
the result of our ministry, written not with ink
but with the Spirit of the living God,
not on tablets of stone but on tablets of human hearts.
2 Corinthians 3:2, 3

Dedication
To Barry

My kind and gentle husband who loved God and his neighbor …
You were always my wonderful friend.
I will always love you.

Praise for *Penned Without Ink* . . .

Honest. Heart-rending. Helpful. Hope-filled. Sarah's narrative masterfully describes the shock, confusion, and struggle to recover from a fiery chain-reaction collision that claimed four lives and injured twenty-five. In the aftermath, she faced life-and-death issues that challenged her firsthand and gave her a new appreciation of grace. Having survived two head-on collisions and numerous close calls in foggy, icy conditions, I'm touched by Sarah's artistic attention to detail, coupled with insights framed by the eternal arch of God writing His story in each of our lives. What a treasure for anyone facing life's perplexing problems.

~ Patricia Souder
Writer and Former Director of
Montrose Christian Writers Conference

I have heard people say over the years that "the only Bible some people will read is your life." If that is true, the Phillips family story has given those who know them an opportunity to see God at work in their lives on a daily basis. I have had the privilege of having a front seat in their story, a story of heartache, grace, and redemption. A must-read.

~ Frank Passetti
Missionary with Youth for Christ in Northeast Pennsylvania

Painful experiences often bring depth and authenticity to the work of great writers. Such is the case with author, Sarah Phillips, who—given a difficult assignment by an all-wise God—writes with "the pen of a ready writer" (Psalm 45:1). Sarah has written an emotionally charged story that embodies the wisdom of Francois Fenelon of the 17th century: "The Great Physician who sees in me what I cannot see, knows exactly where to place the knife. He cuts swift and deep into my innermost being, exposing me for who I really am; but pain is only felt where there is life, and where there is life is just the place where death is needed most. Except a grain of wheat falls into the ground and dies, it abides alone; but if it dies, it will bring forth much fruit." *Penned Without Ink* is a book that you can't read and remain the same.

~ Mark Hamby
President, Lamplighter Ministries International

When Sarah shared how God had been writing her story at our conference a few years ago, I was excited to learn that she was putting that story into book form. As much as I knew that her testimony of God's faithfulness through trauma would touch other women's hearts, I was even more delighted to find that this book would turn out to be so personal—a way for me to see how God is also writing MY story and how I can trust Him from the beginning to the end and all the time between.

~Diane Lytle
Director of LYFE (Living Your Faith Everyday) Women's Conference

You don't have to be the overly compliant good girl who needs permission to follow God's lead into the unknown to be impacted by this book, but *oh,* if you are—what a challenge awaits you! I walked away renewed by the fact that my story is indeed *Penned Without Ink.*

~ Sherry Boykin
Author of *But-Kickers: Growing Your Faith Bigger than Your "But!"*

Knowing Sarah personally—having had children in school together and being members of the same church—gave me, in my thinking, some ownership in her story. I started reading *Penned Without Ink,* envisioning Sarah as a contemporary hero of faith in my mind. But Sarah did not let me. As I read her story, I realized *she* makes God the Hero. I love how she brings God into the story as the main character over and over. This book makes me not just appreciate the Phillips family and God's work in their lives but makes me see God's work in my own. A must-read I am going to pass on.

~ Darlene Smith, RN

Penned Without Ink is a powerful account of finding grace and hope in the midst of suffering. As I spent time with Dr. Barry and Sarah Phillips, I witnessed how the faith that is expressed in these pages was manifested in their daily lives. I would recommend this book to anyone who is trying to find God's providence in the midst of a painful and difficult situation.

~ Joseph Parle, PhD
Academic Dean of the College of Biblical Studies in Houston, TX

Sarah's book, *Penned Without Ink: Trusting God to Write Your Story*, surprised me! I knew it would tell the story of the accident, which in and of itself is compelling. What I didn't expect in its few pages is how effectively it would weave in and explore the deep things of God such as His sovereignty and eternal purposes for suffering. Nor did I anticipate the invitation at the end of each chapter to personally engage (and sometimes wrestle) with the Lover of my soul and the One who has so intricately written my own story. Who should read this book? Every person who needs to be reminded of God's steadfast faithfulness in the midst of the peaks and valleys of their own stories. I guess that would include all of us.

~**Darlene Kordic**
Founding Director of Word of God Speak Ministries
Author of *God's Perspective When Life Hurts*
Missionary with BEE World

Tragedy is common to human existence, but few are those who have learned to tap into God's sustaining grace like Sarah Phillips. Drawing on her own personal experience, Sarah effectively connects the reader with foundational biblical truth, empowering us to stand firm in our faith through our own personal struggles. *Penned Without Ink* shines the piercing light of Scripture into the thick fog of Sarah's personal tragedy, revealing the faithfulness of God in a way sure to change lives.

~ **Rodger Sayre, MD**
FAAFP (Fellow American Academy of Family Physicians)

Sarah shares her story with vulnerability while challenging readers to reflect on how God is crafting their individual stories. I would recommend this book for those who suddenly find themselves in a chapter of life they did not anticipate.

~ **Heather R. Hall, PhD**
Assistant Professor of Counseling,
Licensed Professional Counselor, National Certified Counselor

TABLE OF CONTENTS

INTRODUCTION

ONE STORY.

One story breathed courage into my spirit. One story offered hope beyond the present unknowns. One story served as a grab bar when panic and despair threatened to steal away any strength I had left. Strength I needed to navigate the uninvited trauma that invaded our lives.

Page after page, I read Gracia Burnham's book, *In the Presence of My Enemies*. A halo—screwed into my skull to stabilize my broken neck—kept my head from moving, forcing me to face straight ahead. Compelled to use a hard, straight chair, I sat with my elbows on the dining room table, holding the book at eye level to see the pages ... hungry for a word from God ... searching for a hint of grace.

Gracia Burnham's memoir does not offer soothing verse or warm, wonderful stories. Her account reveals the horrors experienced by two American missionaries taken captive by a Muslim extremist group in the Philippines. For over a year, they and several other hostages were forced to traipse from place to place in the jungle, barely surviving oppression from their captors and the elements. In a rescue attempt, Gracia's husband was shot and killed.

Somewhere between the lines, I discovered a rare kind of strength. I witnessed a faithful God whose awareness and care for His children make a difference in the very worst of times. There at my dining room table, ensconced in my steel halo, I determined that if Gracia Burnham could trust God in a most horrendous chapter of her life story, I could trust Him with this fearful and uncertain chapter of my own.

The power of story touches us all.

Penned Without Ink is a book about story. We each have a distinct, one-of-a-kind life story, penned without ink (2 Corinthians 3:2, 3). Our lives carry a unique slant, one that's exclusive to each of us. Some days reflect God's care and concern in visible, positive ways. We find it easy to count our blessings and feel hopeful about the future. At other times, we discover our plots twisted and troubling. Circumstances seem to plummet from bad to worse. Often, we question God's role in the daily-ness of it all.

What does it mean to trust God? This book helps answer the question. Proverbs 3:5 (AMPC) describes trust this way: "Lean on, trust in, and be confident in the Lord . . ." It carries the idea of leaning "the entire human personality on God in absolute trust and confidence in His power, wisdom, and goodness" (Hebrews 13:7 AMPC). Only God is worthy of our complete trust. His story graces our lives on every page. He never fails.

My firstborn daughter helped me understand my trust relationship with God. When Jana reached preschool age, I placed a fat pencil on her desk along with some paper with big spaces between the lines. With eager determination, Jana gripped the pencil in her chubby little hand and concentrated oh-so-hard, but she could only make meaningless scratches on the page. "Is this my name?" she asked. "I want to write my name."

I knelt down close beside her, placed my hand on top of hers, and slowly guided the pencil, one letter at a time. "There. This is your name. See? J-A-N-A." I pointed to each letter. She looked up at me with a satisfied grin.

"Let's do it again," she begged. This time, she had more confidence. I could feel her hand exert itself against mine, resisting my direction. The letters became distorted and hard to read. Sometimes she trusted me to direct the pencil. Sometimes her independence got the best of her.

Are we the child who lets her hand be guided by the One more capable? Or do we determine to do it all ourselves? *Penned Without Ink: Trusting God to Write Your Story* emphasizes the wisdom of trusting our sovereign, loving God to direct the pencil, His hand upon ours. In each chapter, we discover how we can trust Him, even in the midst of unanswered questions and uncertain steps.

God's Story is woven throughout this book like a timeless, golden thread. I've highlighted scriptural principles and biographies which show His character and faithful involvement in our lives. Take time to reflect on God's love and care for us through *His* story.

Does your faith increase when you read about someone who has worked through painful circumstances and emotions? Mine does. Page by page, I invite you to link arms with me as I share **My Story** of trust, laced with God's comfort and faithfulness.

And now, what about you? My desire is for you to consider **Your Story.** Trusting God day by day lays the foundation for life-change and hope.

Gracia Burnham's words focused my attention on a loving God in the midst of the complicated repercussions of a near-fatal car crash. Through our family's long recovery, God taught me many lessons about trusting Him, one small step at a time. This book reflects much of my journey. I pray it draws you to a deeper trust in the One who offers to write *your* story with infinite wisdom and grace.

PART ONE

AN UNEXPECTED CRISIS
APRIL 5 – MAY 8, 2003

CHAPTER ONE

April 5, 2003
Accident or Providence?

DENSE FOG ENGULFED us as we strained to see past the front end of our car on the Pennsylvania Turnpike. The unexpected, eerie haze on a fair day spiked my pulse and revved up my every nerve. I coached our seventeen-year-old daughter, Sharon, at the wheel. "Slow way down, hon. Put your flashers on."

My apprehensions grew when we tapped what must have been a car ahead of us. Even then, I hung on to hope. *If this is all we hit, we'll be okay.*

I turned to check on five-year-old Elisabeth in the back seat. In that instant, a crushing blow from behind convulsed us back and forth like rag dolls. Elisabeth's legs flew up. My husband, Barry, in the seat beside her, clutched his sides as if in agony. Sickening terror seized me as the life-shattering impact snuffed out hope like a gust of wind chokes a flame on a moonless night.

Fire. Explosions. Screams. Scraping metal. These were the terrifying sounds that pierced the murky mist around us. Only one thought beat like a drum in my mind: *We have to get out of the car. Out of the car. Out …*

In the News

The newspaper called it "the worst accident on the nation's oldest toll road since June 20, 1998, … Four people were killed and 25 were injured … in a pair of fiery chain-reaction collisions on a fog-shrouded, mountaintop section of the Pennsylvania Turnpike …" A few hundred feet from the turnpike, Sam Blizzard, owner of Sam's Mountain Auction, reported, "I heard people screaming and cars banging together—screaming, hollering, banging and explosions." Sixty-five miles of toll road had to be shut down for twelve hours.[1]

If the Lord Wills

There's a reason an accident is called an *accident*. No one traveling the turnpike that fateful morning anticipated a life-changing catastrophe. Caught in the intensity of the moment, each driver did his or her best to navigate the fog. Some could have used better judgment, but the damage occurred without intention. I never blamed any of our fellow travelers but often prayed for the faceless names linked to numbered vehicles in the police report.

It all happened so fast—tragedy, loss, injury, grief, uncertainty—wrapped up in one brief moment of time. Each life ... forever altered.

Life is fragile. In the first century, James wrote, "You do not know what will happen tomorrow. For what is your life? It is even a vapor that appears for a little time and then vanishes away. Instead you ought to say, '*If the Lord wills, we shall live and do this or that.*'"[2] When we began our trip, God knew each detail of what lay ahead. For reasons known only to Him, in accordance with His will ... we lived.

Road Warriors

At the crash site, we knew only what we ourselves experienced. How could we comprehend the enormity of the multi-car collisions, fires, injuries, and deaths, let alone the implications of it all? Our car was rear-ended twice. After the second and most horrendous impact to the back left side—and my desperate thoughts to exit the car—only a few spotty recollections lodged themselves in my muddled mind. Yet God placed someone at the scene who later filled in some of the blanks.

With her two friends, a young woman named Bethan was headed in the opposite direction on the turnpike. After fog enveloped the highway, she parked her car—fifth in a line of stopped vehicles—across the median from our crash. With zero visibility, the women could only hear the crashes and explosions, the screams of victims, and the screech of tires and metal on the other side. Within a short time, the fog lifted, revealing a panorama of mangled, burning wreckage. Before rescue workers arrived, Bethan and her friends brought blankets from their car to help keep accident victims warm. Elisabeth, Sharon, and I were among the people they aided.

Weeks later, I phoned Bethan to thank her for her kindness and courage. "Do you know how we got out of the car?" I asked her.

"You must have gotten yourselves out," she said. "We saw you walking away from the road, down the hill in the ditch. We called you back. You were carrying your little girl, and your older daughter clung to your arm. She seemed very confused."

They called us back …

I could just picture my motherly self urging Sharon and Elisabeth out of the car, trying to flee the immediate danger. Did God send these friends to keep us from wandering off, hidden from the help we so desperately needed?

Bethan told me Elisabeth didn't cry but remained quiet as long as she snuggled next to me. She wanted to be held. I complained of neck pain. No one knew which car belonged to us.

I do remember lying on a red plaid blanket between the two girls. A woman, later known by our family as "the nice lady with the white hair," sat beside us. Bethan offered the use of her cell phone. Slowly, and with great concentration, I gave my parents' phone number, but she or the lady did the talking. I didn't possess enough coherence to wonder how the news affected them, nor did I have the sense to inquire about my husband or even understand the surrounding bedlam. Elisabeth's little eyes and ears absorbed the most—people yelling, an ambulance nearby, and fires burning all around. Anything to do with fire, including smoke alarms and fire trucks, triggered intense fear in her for months afterward.

Apparently, I gave Bethan my name. When her pastor requested prayer for us at her church the next morning, she recognized our names and soon connected me as a friend of her best friend's aunt.

In the course of our conversation, I asked how this experience affected her.

"Well, I didn't drive for a while," she answered quietly.

Her response sobered me. Trauma is trauma, no matter

how it presents itself or at which end a person finds herself. Bethan's willingness to revisit the horror of the scene with the accompanying emotions demonstrated kindness and courage. Talking with her helped me get a better picture of what I could not remember so I could better process the whole incident. I thanked her from the bottom of my heart.

The September 2003 issue of *Reader's Digest* gives more insight into the twenty-three car pile-up. An article titled "Road Warriors" tells the story of how the women's rugby team from Indiana University of Pennsylvania risked their lives to help. Two of the team members found their way to the median and witnessed another chain-reaction crash, this time in the westbound lanes. "While glass, metal chunks and tire fragments flew, the two women stood in the median strip, waving their arms and yelling at passing cars. 'Stop!' they screamed. 'There's a crash!' But few vehicles even slowed."[3]

Meanwhile, farther back, with fires raging around them, their teammates helped medics lift people onto backboards and stretchers, apply neck braces and bandages, and hook up oxygen masks. A couple of girls crawled through oil and glass to rescue an elderly man and his wife pinned in their car. Two others wrapped a man's bleeding head in a T-shirt, and some reassured the injured as they waited to be taken to the hospital in ambulances. After three hours, the team gathered together to pray for the victims.[4] On the one-year anniversary of the accident, I wrote a letter to thank them for their outstanding courage and assistance.

My last vague memory of the scene on the highway found me lying in an ambulance with the girls by my side, wondering what had happened to my husband.

Surrounded by Grace

Remembering the crash site reminds me of an old Sunday school lesson. An angry king sent a great army by night to surround a prophet's residence. At dawn's light, overwhelming panic seized the prophet's servant when he saw the innumerable number of enemy troops, horses, and chariots surrounding them. But the prophet stayed calm and unafraid. When God opened the servant's eyes, he saw the hills full of horses and chariots of fire all around—the army of the Lord. They had been surrounded by God's protection the whole time.[5]

Words cannot fully describe the frenzied scene of the pile-up on the turnpike. Like Elisha's servant, we found ourselves surrounded. Surrounded by an army of charred and twisted vehicles, shattered glass, and broken bodies. Overwhelming distress and fear seized both victims and responders alike.

Looking back, I have to believe we were also surrounded by God's army—an army of grace. The fading fog. A young woman named Bethan who called us back to the scene. The lady who sat with us. The offer of a cell phone. The rugby team. The medical personnel. Grace-givers every step of the way. And the promise of God's presence in the midst of it all.

Uncertain Days

After initial evaluations at small local hospitals, helicopters life-flighted the four of us to three different hospitals. Sharon and I went to Conemaugh Memorial Medical Center in Johnstown, Pennsylvania. Sharon sustained minimal physical injuries and was released within a day or two. In my room, tubes, wires, and monitors enveloped the bed. Intubated, I lay in traction to stabilize a broken neck.

Little Elisabeth, accompanied by no one but a medical worker, spent the night at Pittsburgh Children's Hospital before her discharge into my parents' care the next day.

At Altoona Hospital, forty-five minutes from Johnstown, Barry's life became a flickering candle in the darkness of a coma. His diagnosis included a nearly-severed spleen and, worse, a traumatic brain injury (TBI).

For me, the hours and days dragged. Sleepless nights brought drug-induced hallucinations, disorientation, and bits of conversations with God, who seemed far away, yet strangely present.

The welfare of my girls troubled me. Their physical injuries would heal in time, but what about the emotional repercussions of this trauma? Their dad ... would he make it? If he did, the initial prognosis relayed to me from his doctors looked grim. Whatever lay ahead would present difficult adjustments for all three of them. Our oldest daughter, Jana, left her college studies to help us. I feared Sharon would carry guilt after facing an impossible situation as a young driver. And Elisabeth, still so little. I *had* to pull through. *I had* to recover. They needed me.

Skilled surgeons performed two delicate operations seven days apart and outfitted me with a metal halo to stabilize my neck so my vertebrae could heal after C3 and C4 had been fused. Two pins screwed into my forehead and two more behind my ears forced my head and neck into an uncompromising position. The halo also included a brace that encircled my trunk. The first time the nurses tried to help me stand after surgery, I could not balance. It felt like a staggering fifty pounds on my head. How would I manage this halo for three whole months?

Three weeks post-accident, and still unable to walk, I was transferred to a rehab facility within a few miles of where Barry still lay immobile and unresponsive. Social workers arranged transportation so I could finally see him. My heart pounded as I rode the elevator in a high-backed wheelchair and approached his room. His pale, still form, entwined with tubes and wires, drew me to his side.

I loved this man.

I reached for his needled hand. "Barry," I whispered. "It's Sarah. I'm here with you now. Please come back to us. We love you. We need you …"

Only the monotonous murmur of the breathing machine in the otherwise silent room answered me. Suddenly, the responsibility of so many decisions and uncertainties weighed heavily on my halo-laden shoulders.

That day, I had no idea what the future held for our family. Questions swirled in my mind—questions with no answers. But over the next weeks and months, God graciously surrounded me with His faithfulness as I desperately sought to trust Him with the rest of our story.

CHAPTER TWO

Perfect Stories?

THE EVENTS SURROUNDING the car crash molded and changed my life forever. It didn't seem to me to be a "perfect story." But with time and love, God taught me that even a near-fatal tragedy could become perfect in His hands.

My author friends and I love to write. But our words are far from perfect. When we meet together to critique each other's writing, each of us has spent long hours since our last meeting spinning story lines. And we often read rewrites. Why? Because a writer doesn't get it right the first time. Our first drafts sound disjointed, lacking the smooth flow of ideas and the pluck of just the right word. The key to good writing is rewriting.

Unlike me—or any other author—God writes perfect stories because He is perfect. Because He is faultless and whole. Only God qualifies as the ultimate "author and *perfecter* of our faith."[1]

History is His Story

God's eternal story begins in Genesis and has its climax in Revelation. God lovingly draws our individual lives into His ultimate plan.

I find the Old Testament full of accounts that illustrate how a perfect God reveals Himself and His perfect plan. Each story unveils His love for the children of earth and His promise of a coming Savior. At just the right time, in His grand plot for the universe, He sent His Son so we may enjoy a lasting relationship with Him.

Jesus told parables to teach kingdom truths. People flocked to hear Him teach spiritual insights, share anecdotes, and answer questions. Jesus framed the right story to fit each need—all the while nudging His listeners to find their place in His design for the ages.

God's Perfect Character

God never asks us to trust a vague idea. He reveals Himself as a God with specific attributes, a God who personally engages in our lives. He invites us to observe His perfect and credible character, to know Him ... and to trust Him.

I followed the life of an ancient king who experienced God's dependable nature and goodness firsthand. David, whose biography is recorded in the Old Testament books of 1 and 2 Samuel, penned many of the Psalms. He writes, "As for God, his way is perfect; the word of the LORD is flawless. He is a shield for all who take refuge in him. It is God who arms me with strength and makes my way perfect."[2] *Perfect* carries the idea of complete, entire, without blemish.

Throughout his life as a shepherd and king, David filled his journals with poetry and song. They overflow with imagery that personalizes God's character. Who better to portray God as a shield than one who leaped out of the way when King Saul tried to pin him to the wall with a spear? David relished the fact that the God whose way is perfect made *his* way perfect.

I reflected on David's thumbs-up, *perfect* moments: The afternoon Samuel anointed him king. His victory over Goliath. His friendship with Jonathan. His final coronation as king over a united nation.

But David's life didn't always fit my finite definition of *perfect*. What about the scorn of his brothers? The years as a fugitive? The loss of his first wife? His choice to commit adultery with Bathsheba and murder her husband? The death of his baby son, and later, the demise of Absalom who attempted to pull the kingdom out from under him?

David's prayers reveal deep emotion in the midst of both celebration and difficulty. Sometimes his troubles were linked to his poor choices. But not always. The prophet Samuel and the apostle Paul named him a man after God's own heart.[3] No matter what David faced, over and over again, he came back to this: "But I trust in you, O LORD; I say, 'You are my God.' ... How great is your goodness ..."[4]

Reading deeper, these words in Psalm 31 do not reflect

celebration. David finds himself in distress. Broken with grief. Wrestling with rejection and fear. Just like you and me when life takes a wrong turn. And yet, with intention, he clings to the only One whose goodness imparts courage, strength, and hope.

How did David learn to have confidence in a perfect God he'd never seen? How could he claim a *perfect* story? His prayers express a deep understanding of God's ways. His relationship with God portrays more than a forced ritual. He often took time to meditate on the Scriptures. To talk to God. To listen.

I discovered that the perfect way of Israel's shepherd-king depended more on God's love, personal protection, and care than on David's circumstances. He experienced God's infinite faithfulness firsthand in times of victory *and* defeat. He came to know the author of his life intimately.

A Perfect Plotline

All of history reflects God's story. He has a thoughtful plan for your story and mine. His flawless nature allows us to experience His faithfulness up close in the extremes of victory and defeat. All He writes on the pages of heaven and earth never needs to be edited.

Yet—like our car crash—life's offerings can resemble a word search more than a neatly ordered manuscript. We began our car trip on a fair day with high clouds, clear visibility, and dry roads. Dense fog dropped out of nowhere. More than twenty vehicles crashed, leaving a stretch of mangled wreckage on the turnpike. And just minutes after the last car careened off the highway—even before help arrived—the fog lifted.

I'm surrounded by friends experiencing equally sobering circumstances. An illness has left Tim with many debilitating symptoms. Laura faces a high-stress job by day and a lonely apartment by night. Childhood memories still haunt Sherry, who witnessed domestic violence, experienced abuse, and lost her dad to a drug overdose. Another friend, whom I'll call Christine, finds herself reeling from her husband's unfaithfulness.

Perfect stories? We feel conflicted when we brush against accounts like these. How *does* the dark side of life fit with God's perfect ways? We'd rather embrace the miracles, the healings, the it'll-never-happen conversions, and the transformed relationships. Instead, problems often overwhelm us, and we struggle with disappointment, pain, and unanswered questions. Has God forgotten us? Our feelings may mushroom into clouds of doubt, obscuring the truths we hold dear.

Like David, I'm learning that my perfect plotline has more to do with God's character than with my circumstances. More to do with His loving and consistent involvement in the midst of unsettling situations than with my idea of resolution. More to do with God, who watches and weighs all that happens, even when I can't see Him.

He makes all the difference in this fallen world.

In a poem of thanksgiving, David once again put pen to parchment. "The LORD will perfect that which concerns me; Your mercy, O LORD, endures forever; Do not forsake the works of Your hands."[5]

Here, *perfect* means to end or complete. Another translation puts it this way: "The LORD will fulfill his purpose for me; …"[6] God always finishes His stories. He doesn't leave us an unfinished manuscript in a forgotten file. He never abandons us.[7]

Have you noticed that those who possess depth and wisdom have gone through difficult, often severe trials? They're the ones we go to when we're struggling. We grab their books off the shelf. Their stories bolster our faith when we're in trouble. Why is it that pain and loss often initiate spiritual and personal growth?

Perhaps it's because we have nowhere to look but up. James 4:6 reminds us that God gives His sweet grace to the lowly. In author Ken Gire's words, "Whatever happens in our lives to humble us is, in the long run, a good thing, because it paves the road over which the grace of God comes to us."[8]

Second Corinthians 12:7-10 gives us a grace story, one we can pull off the shelf when we feel weak and low. Paul had a condition that continually hampered his person and ministry. He called it a "thorn" in his flesh. He begged God to take his prickly problem away.

"But [God] said to me, 'My grace (favor, loving-kindness, and mercy[9]) is sufficient for you …'" It's enough.

Grace makes me think of frosting. Before I begin icing a cake, I want to make sure I have more than enough frosting. I wouldn't want to find myself spreading it thinner and thinner without reaching to the edges of my cake.

God is never short on grace. He spreads it over us in lavish amounts. It's thick enough to cover every dark corner and every inch, all the way to the ragged edges of our lives.

But there's more: "My strength (My miraculous power, My might, My abundant ability [10]) is made perfect (fulfilled, complete[11]) in weakness."[12] *The Amplified Bible* says, "My strength *and* power ... *show themselves most effective* in [your] weakness."

We get sick, stressed, frustrated. The good things in our lives seem to be crowded out by calamities and inner anguish. We feel weak, but in these very moments, Christ promises His miraculous power and strength will be made perfect. Our difficulties don't necessarily get easier. But we have to believe the grace He promises is sufficient—enough—just like ample frosting on a cake, spread over every corner and edge of today.

Tim's wife, Jan, writes, "I am learning more and more that God is the Master of taking the awful thing in our lives and turning it into something good, positive, and beautiful."[13] She goes on to share how God has helped them, often through the kindness of others.

Laura demonstrates integrity at work and blesses many with her warm friendship.

Sherry, on her blog, shares, "... without [those childhood experiences] I'd probably never find myself writing or speaking about anything meaningful. My outer shell may reveal trauma, but my inner self, my soul, sings for my Savior—for what He did *not* withhold, for the grit through which my story shines, for my *all rightness* despite what is clearly not right ... over and over again."[14]

Christine confides, "The past four years have been the most difficult and humbling of my life, yet the relationship I have with God has grown closer, sweeter, and more dependent."

Accident or providence?

A.W. Tozer writes, "To the child of God, there is no such thing as an accident. ... Accidents may indeed appear to befall him and misfortune stalk his way; but ... we cannot read the secret script of God's hidden providence ..."[15]

Every day, God gifts us with His presence. In the midst of imperfect and unpredictable pages, He invites us to know Him in a deeper way. When surrounded by loss, heartache, and disappointment, He draws us to take comfort in His refuge. He calls us to remember His impeccable character and His faithful track record. He beckons us to experience His credibility and the relevancy of His truth. The perfect Master Writer has committed Himself to complete His perfect work in each of us. He desires to guide the pencil because, unlike any earthbound writer, God writes perfect stories ... even when they take place in the fog on the Pennsylvania Turnpike.

Your Story

God's writing is perfect, and He invites you to trust Him. Prayerfully think through what holds you back from trusting God completely with every detail of your story. What fears or doubts plague your thinking? What unanswered questions do you have? What areas of resistance hold a grip on your life? Meditate on what you've learned in chapters one and two about God's character and His commitment to accomplish His perfect work in you. Write a prayer or a story of trust. Refer to Psalm 138:8 and Philippians 1:6.

CHAPTER THREE

Behold My Hands

REMEMBERING A STORY is a little like taking a box of photos off the shelf, lifting the lid, and spreading the pictures out on a table. Each one, a moment frozen in time. One by one, we pick them up, study them, compare them. Often, the subjects overlap or the same scene has been captured from another perspective. We can't always place the pictures—or the story—in a linear sequence. Rather, they represent multiple layers of experience. They illustrate the observations and perceptions of both participants and bystanders. As we sift through the photos, we recall each occasion. The emotions come rushing back. And as time passes, we try to comprehend how these events fit with the others in our lives. We try to understand the purpose.

I remember many of the images surrounding the car crash and our recovery. Family members and friends, like Bethan, have also helped me piece events together, creating a story of faith. Another significant snapshot follows.

According to my parents, a series of phone calls throughout the afternoon sent them scurrying to find luggage, maps, and hospital addresses. Five hours away, their daughter's life hung in uncertainty. They knew only bits and pieces: a multi-car pile-up, life flights, the family split up in different hospitals. Trauma.

After a grueling drive, Dad and Mom found my hospital room. Their breath caught as they stared at the tubes, wires, and monitors that enveloped my bed. My face, stitched and swollen, made my identity impossible. Could this be their precious daughter? As the horrific impact washed over them, Mom finally recognized one thing—my hands.

She knew them well. My tiny baby fingers had wrapped

around her strong ones. She and Dad clutched my tiny hands in theirs to keep me from stumbling on my little toddler legs. They taught me to tie my shoelaces and write the ABCs. They held my hands when I lay sick with fever and when I thought my heart would break. They watched them play the flute, show off an engagement ring, swaddle their grandchildren, and serve special dinners for family celebrations.

Standing beside me in the ICU that night, my parents again clasped my hands. In the days ahead they would hold my hands to steady my steps during my long recovery. They would press courage and hope into my heart by giving my hands a squeeze while we all struggled to understand the redeeming value in our circumstances.

Like my parents, a man from another century struggled to recognize and confirm the identity of someone precious to him. Thomas failed to see much evidence of Jesus' resurrection. Even after the other disciples exclaimed, "We have seen the Lord!" skepticism kept him in disbelief. "Unless I see the nail marks in his hands and put my finger where the nails were, and put my hand into his side, I will not believe it."[1]

Thomas had witnessed the hands of Jesus in action many times. Likely, Thomas watched Jesus take little children up in His arms, put His hands on them, and bless them. He observed Jesus' busy hands preparing a meal for five thousand from a young boy's lunch. He witnessed the Lord heal the eyes of two blind men who immediately received their sight. Time after time, a touch from Jesus offered courage, healing, and hope to the sick and sinner alike.

Later, Thomas felt Christ's palms and fingers wash the dust and grime from his feet, a lesson in service and humility. He ate bread broken by the hands of Jesus at the Passover. He knew all too well how soldiers pounded spikes through Jesus' hands and feet before lifting Him up to die an excruciating death on a Roman cross.

The questions churning through Thomas's mind must have mocked the emptiness he felt inside. Now what? And they wanted him to believe Jesus was alive?

Eight long days passed. As the disciples gathered together behind closed doors, their voices murmured softly. Who had seen their risen Master? Perhaps Thomas crossed his arms and eyed them from a distance. As some of them recalled the statements Jesus made before His death, understanding began to brighten their spirits.[2]

Suddenly, Jesus stood in their midst. "Peace be with you!" Thomas's eyes must have opened wide as his heart pounded out of his chest and color flushed his cheeks. Jesus spoke directly to him. "Put your finger here; see my hands. Reach out your hand and put it into my side. Stop doubting and believe."

Recognizing Jesus, Thomas could only exclaim, "My Lord and my God!"[3] At that moment, he doubted no more. All Christ's claims to deity made sense. The scars in the Savior's hands and side proclaimed an eternal redeeming value: "... that whoever believes in him shall not perish but have eternal life."[4]

Years have passed since my dad and mom visited my bedside, yet I still find myself standing beside Thomas in the inner room of my heart. Like him, I often long to see more tangible evidence of how God works a seeming tragedy for good.

The Unfolding of a Story

I remember one snapshot of our journey after another. The first day five-year-old Elisabeth could visit me, she shrank back, apprehension in her eyes, which were blackened from a concussion. Besides the halo, hospital bed, and IVs in the room, swelling and stitches still crisscrossed my face. How I longed to hold her in my arms. Instead, I used a puppet to play with her from a distance. Finally, love triumphed over fear. The first time she cautiously crawled into bed beside me, I blinked back tears of joy.

Another picture shows me choking. I couldn't eat. The operation affected my swallowing, as the surgeon had fused two vertebrae by going through the *front* of my neck. Finally, pureeing my food seemed to work. Even then, I was too weak to feed myself. As I grew stronger, the hospital staff taught me eating strategies to keep me from choking and gave me applesauce to get my pills down.

More snapshots. There was the morphine pump. The bedsore on the back of my head from lying on my back for so long. The muscle spasms. The pain of cracked ribs when the nurses rolled me onto my side to change the sheets. The parade of labs, tests, and x-rays. The day the MRI revealed what x-rays could not: on top of broken neck vertebrae, I had also sustained a 40 percent shattering of my L1 vertebra. This necessitated a second major surgery. While doctors figured out what to do next, I lay confined in a Roto-Rest bed that rocked back and forth continuously for three or four days to aid circulation and prevent blood clots.

The morning of my second operation, Jana and Sharon came early to see me off. As I looked into their eyes, I wondered what I could say to my precious daughters who had to be so brave. I knew the risks but tried to stay upbeat for their sakes. In the OR, just before the nine-hour procedure began, I had to remain awake while doctors placed a tube down my throat. Panic seized me as I gagged and struggled to breathe before they finally put me under.

Later, the surgeon told me I would need to take medication for pain and inflammation for the rest of my life, doubling the dose in cold weather. He said the trauma had added twenty years to my age—a nice way of informing me of my diminished life expectancy. "And don't lift anything," he added before leaving the room.

I just wanted to get out of bed.

The day finally came when I clumsily clung to a walker and took my first steps. My mother's smile gave me courage as I shuffled toward the window. There, I looked out onto a busy world that had gone on without me. I reached for the warmth of the first sunshine I had seen in nearly three weeks.

Soon after, I transferred to HealthSouth Rehabilitation Hospital in Altoona. But I had little to wear. My halo, with four metal rods attached to a chest brace, prevented me from wearing a regular shirt. I had only one peasant-style pajama top that worked. The nurses helped my family order special T-shirts with Velcro openings on both sides.

Before Jana left for Target to pick up some pants for me, I asked her to buy me a razor and tweezers. At that point I didn't worry about the blood thinners for a blot clot I had developed and the fact that, if I nicked myself, I'd be hard-pressed to stop the bleeding. Determined—despite the halo and wheelchair—I carefully managed to shave every last hair off my legs from my knees down. Accomplishing this simple task somehow lifted my chin a little higher as I counted sets of leg lifts and pushed my walker around the therapy room.

In each snapshot, an overwhelming concern for my husband formed the backdrop. Jana took a couple of days to drive home and shop for a nursing facility. She chose the perfect place, but I felt sorry that she, a twenty-year-old college student, had to do it. Once I transferred to HealthSouth, Jana, along with Barry's brother and sister-in-law who had come from Michigan to help, spent their days with Barry and their evenings with me. Every night we strategized about who I should contact the next day between therapy sessions and what questions I should ask about Barry's future care. At last, we had a plan in place. I would come home on May 7th, and Barry would transfer to the nursing home on May 8th.

But the morning I was to leave, I pulled a back muscle. Even with high-power meds, I couldn't move without pain that left me breathless. Yet another x-ray revealed no damage, so they discharged me. Four hours later, tears slipped down my cheeks as I hobbled through the back door into our dining room. Thirty-two days late, the girl whose favorite place is home finally returned from vacation.

Picture after picture, our story continued to unfold. Barry and I fought long and hard to recover. Change and uncertainty often made the way confusing and obscure. At times, we responded with firm steps of faith and sound choices. At other times, doubt and misjudgment sent us sprawling. This caused physical, emotional, and even spiritual scars.

As Christ continually offers His peace to me, I echo the sentiments of the disciple whose walk of faith began with the words, "My Lord and my God!" With gratitude, I embrace this plan of redemption that His death and resurrection represent. The scars I deserve for my sin rest in His hands.

I'm learning to recognize that every wound, every scar God allows in my life, has an eternal purpose—even when that purpose may not be visible to me now. Yes, there has been growth through the struggle and a new compassion in my focus. I treasure the lessons learned and the insights gained. But when doubts and questions nag in the quiet of the night, and I've lost sight of God's sovereign hand, Jesus' words breathe hope into my heart. "Blessed are those who have not seen and yet have believed."[5]

Today, "we live by faith, not by sight."[6] But someday we will see Jesus Himself, face-to-face. The purpose for the pictures in our story lines will all become clear.

I shall know Him, I shall know Him,
And redeemed by His side I shall stand,
I shall know Him, I shall know Him
By the print of the nails in His hand.[7]
~ Fanny Crosby

CHAPTER FOUR

What's the Point?

FOLLOWING THE TURNPIKE collision, questions, uncertainties, and what seemed like pointless suffering filled our days. But here and there, in the midst of the darkness, I caught glimpses of grace ... of light. As time went on, I began to look for them. And the more I looked, the more I found. These pictures of hope heightened my awareness that God had a purpose for our circumstances.

After six years of trying to get our story down on paper, I understand a little about the role of purpose in writing. As writers, we strive to have a reason for every character, every event, and every idea. We may write a stellar paragraph, but if it doesn't hold a significant connection to the whole story, it has no purpose. We cross it out. Delete it. *Is this part necessary?* we ask ourselves. *What's the point?*

When we write or do anything "on purpose," we have a reason, a goal, an intended outcome in mind.

God writes our stories with purpose.

There's no mistake when it comes to our family trees, personalities, and talents. We can never label our experiences, joys, and tears as inadvertent or accidental. They're all part of the *Table of Contents* God has outlined for us. All part of His story.

Sometimes we see God's rationale in the moment. At other times, it takes years before we glimpse the reasons for our circumstances. Often, God seems to place our sentences and paragraphs in random combinations. We can't see any explanation for our circumstances and losses. We wonder, *What's the point?*

In the dark, we cling to God's promises in faith. We choose to believe God and His Word *without* seeing. And then sometimes God graciously offers us a peek into His purposes. He allows us to see a ray of hope ... a light that draws us into His warm embrace.

God's Loving Purposes

Throughout my recovery, it helped me to remember that, from the very beginning, God's plan has been driven by His loving purposes. He has a reason for everything He does.

Tucked in the prayers and prophecies of the Old Testament, I discovered the certainty of God's purposes. Isaiah made it a point to relay God's messages word for word. "'Surely, as I have planned, so it will be, and as I have purposed, so it will stand.' ... For the LORD Almighty has purposed, and who can thwart him? His hand is stretched out, and who can turn it back?"[1]

"'I am God, and there is no other; ... My purpose will stand, and I will do all that I please. ... What I have said, that will I bring about; what I have planned, that will I do.'"[2]

The Almighty is never haphazard. He's purposeful.

It comforts me to know that not only do God's eternal purposes stand, but He includes me in those purposes.

Purposeful Stories

I have read many stories that point to the purposes of God—Abraham, David, and Paul's stories among them.

Abraham waited twenty-five long years for God's promise of a son to be fulfilled. While he waited, his faith grew strong. He became more convinced than ever that God, indeed, "was able *and* mighty to keep His word *and* to do what He had promised."[3] I prayed our struggles would not cause us to lose our faith but would strengthen it.

God intentionally allowed wild animals to prey on David's flock of sheep to serve as a training ground so he would have confidence in the living God to defeat Goliath. The lions and bears served a practical and divine purpose. Corrie ten Boom's words gave me a parallel perspective. "Every experience God gives us, every person He puts in our lives is the perfect preparation for the future that only He can see."[4] Could I believe that nothing in our family story would be wasted?

As an inmate chained to a guard around the clock, the apostle Paul took the opportunity to share Christ on every shift.[5] His prison time served to propel God's story to yet another people group, Rome's imperial guard. Through Paul, God chose to further His kingdom in unexpected ways. Perhaps—though I felt imprisoned by our circumstances and linked to a lifetime of limitations—God would ask me to bless those I never would have connected with otherwise.

Like these men, I wanted my faith to grow, my trials to fortify the future, and my influence to draw people to Christ.

Stories of Light

We will never know the full extent of God's purposes for allowing the car wreck—not in this life. As the years slip by, I look back on our experience with more perspective. But at this stage in our story, I had only the images of light along the way to bring me closer to trust a purposeful God who promises His "present *and* well-proved help in trouble."[6]

I remember the grace-sightings, times when we caught a small glimpse of His presence ... when it seemed as though He sent special messengers to reassure us of His love.

We cherish "pictures" of Jana and my parents, the first to respond to a series of phone calls bearing heart-wrenching news and often conflicting reports. Barry's siblings, Maxine and Gary, left their jobs and homes in Michigan to stay with him in Altoona. His niece, Rayan, and her fiancé, Peter, also came. Gary and his wife, Karen, retrieved our luggage, embedded with broken glass, from our car at the junkyard. Karen cared for Elisabeth and looked out for Sharon in the guesthouse in Johnstown so my parents could stay with me and follow my ever-changing condition. I appreciated those who sat with me, along with our pastors and a few others who visited. Their coming broke up the tense, tedious days. Shortly before I returned home, my sister flew in from her missionary work in Africa to help in any way she could.

We remember snapshots of those who blessed us with their gifts of foresight and thoughtfulness. Pastor Frank, the assistant pastor of our church, arranged for my parents and the girls to stay at a guest house near the hospital in Johnstown. Our church paid the bill.

God listened to the precious prayers of an unseen support group from all over the world. Years later, people still tell me, "We prayed for you." Many sent cards with messages of support and encouragement. I kept them all. A few sent gifts of money. Not one bill went unpaid.

The surgeon who fused my neck happened to be a Christian from Ethiopia. My parents appreciated not only his expertise during the six-hour surgery but also his compassion and concern. He confirmed the fracture of the C3, C4, C5, and C6 vertebrae and his fusion of C3 and C4. He also noted a miracle: in spite of the extensive trauma, my spinal cord had remained intact. In His grace, God spared me from becoming paralyzed. Both surgeons excelled in their field and did a wonderful job putting me back together.

A few times, Sharon and I watched the hospital channel of inspirational music set to beautiful scenery. She curled up in the bed beside me, and, all the while, tears wet our cheeks as the familiar hymns touched our hearts and offered a glimmer of hope.

We spent Easter in Johnstown. The hospital nursing staff, out of their own resources, put together Easter baskets for Sharon and Elisabeth. Their everyday kindnesses blessed me and showed me they were pulling for all of us.

When my parents drove home for a quick weekend, they brought my broken glasses to my optician. When he heard about our tragedy, he replaced them at no cost.

The social workers not only made special arrangements to admit me to a rehab facility close to Barry's hospital but went so far as to provide a van for me to see him. They loaded me up, wheelchair and all, dropped me off at the hospital doors, and brought me back almost every afternoon for two weeks.

I will never forget those visits with my husband. Side-by-side, one-way conversations. How long would the coma separate us? Would Barry ever again whisper my name? Squeeze my hand? Hold me close? I treasured the moments we spent together, and I prayed—oh, how I prayed—he would open his eyes and come back to me.

One afternoon I phoned the business manager at the Christian college where Barry served as Vice President for

College Academics and begged him not to cancel our health insurance. I offered to clean bathrooms or do *anything* to pay for our insurance once I recovered. The reassuring voice on the other end of the line promised support and even disability insurance, should we need it.

When the time came, family members transported Sharon, Elisabeth, and me back to the Scranton area. After I left the Johnstown hospital for rehab in Altoona on April 24, nineteen days after the crash, my dad and mom took Sharon and Elisabeth home with them. Thirteen days later, Gary and Karen carefully drove me the four hours home before returning to Michigan. Jana came home about the same time. The next day, an ambulance took Barry to a nursing facility close to home. Finally, we were all in the same geographic area.

These portraits lit the path on which we found ourselves. Without all the people who helped us, our recovery would have been impossible. We will *never* be able to adequately thank these grace-givers. Within God's perfect purposes, they have added light to the pages of our story. Although I didn't know it at the time, I would need these pictures to help me through the dark days ahead.

Eyes of Faith

It helps me to remember that God has a plan and purpose for our family. When His promises seem impossible, He strengthens our faith. He delivers us in life's challenges and equips us for the future. His purposes reach far beyond our particular situation and lead us to draw others to Himself.

Have you found, like me, that it's easier to become focused on your problems than on the grace of God? When we can't see God's purposes with true eyes of faith, we miss the point. Peter offers an eternal perspective: "Now for a little while you may have had to suffer grief in all kinds of trials. These have come so that your faith ... may be proved genuine and may result in praise, glory, and honor when Jesus Christ is revealed."[7] A "great cloud of witnesses" surrounds us with their stories, encouraging us toward perseverance. Their message echoes through the passage of time: "Let us fix our eyes on Jesus, the author and perfecter of our faith, ... so that [we] will not grow weary and lose heart."[8] Every day, God's infinite wisdom shapes His work in our lives. Each picture lays a foundation for the next, and with the right choices, reinforces our confidence in Him. What's the point? We can trust that God has a significant purpose for *all* He writes on the pages of our life stories. And at just the right time—*His* time—He offers us a glimpse of light in the darkness.

Your Story

God is writing your life story with purpose. How does your view of God fit with what is recorded by Isaiah in this chapter? When have you struggled to trust God because you couldn't see His purposes, only to later discover that your faith was strengthened? How have the lions and bears in your life prepared you to overcome your Goliaths? What life experiences have given you opportunities to touch the lives of others in significant ways? Meditate on what you've learned in chapters three and four about God's wise purposes for everything He does. Write a prayer or story of trust. Refer to Romans 8:28; Philippians 2:13; and 1 Peter 1:6, 7.

CHAPTER FIVE

A Deadly Dilemma

GOD WROTE HIS perfect story for us—one with purpose—in the foggy chaos on the Pennsylvania Turnpike. Gradually, I recognized this truth revealed through picture after picture of God's faithfulness. Pictures of light in the darkness.

There's yet another story that needs to be told, one of a husband, a father, a brother, an uncle ... lost in the midnight of a coma. Barry's story.

After Barry was found beside a charred red pickup truck, an ambulance rushed him to the closest medical facility.[1] From there, medics eased him into a waiting helicopter while the pilot ran back to secure another nurse and more blood. As they lifted off, the nurses gave him blood as fast as he lost his own. Within minutes of their arrival at Altoona Hospital, an unnamed surgeon clamped the spurting artery and removed Barry's partially severed spleen. The pilot's quick response and the doctor's skill saved his life.

Protocol dictated a temporary induced coma to allow Barry's body to rest and heal. Besides the obvious, no initial sense of concern accompanied the procedure. They also inserted a stent into his head to drain the fluid collecting on his brain. A respirator supported his breathing.

After several days, they cut back on the sedating drugs, but the coma continued. No one could rouse him. Was it because of extensive injury to the brainstem which controls, among other functions, breathing, heart rate, and wakefulness? Jana and Maxine along with Gary and Rayan took turns keeping vigil by Barry's bedside. They talked to him. They held his hand. And they prayed.

Multiple points of view made this traumatic scenario complicated and emotionally charged. After reading the results of Barry's tests and brain scans, the brain specialist felt that with all the trauma, Barry's condition was too far gone. "A one-in-a-million chance," he stated bluntly. He'd seen it before. Humanly speaking, his speculations probably reflected a realistic prognosis. He recommended the family seriously consider authorizing the removal of the respirator that kept him alive. In other words, pull the plug.

Soon after, the family heard from the original surgeon. He felt the operation had been successful, and time would reveal the ultimate outcome. "Nothing has to be decided now," he said with compassion.

Relatives, already under the duress of a nightmare, couldn't agree on the best course of action. One opinion, reflective of a lengthy conversation with the neurologist, suggested that disconnecting the respirator would allow God to do His will, rather than using mechanical means to extend Barry's life. Another perspective insisted that God had provided doctors with medical expertise, and the added time on the respirator could be beneficial. Family at both hospitals grappled with a deadly dilemma that tore them apart. They knew Barry wouldn't want to be kept alive this way. Everyone felt understandably upset. Conversations grew heated. Who could know the right answers at a time like this?

Ultimately, the decision could only be made by one person. Me. In another hospital, just days after the crash with a major surgery the next day, I faced the decision of my life.

Despite protests of "We can't tell her this now," I finally heard the news third-hand. By the time the message reached me, it was more a question of *when* to stop the breathing machine than *if*. Perhaps my compliant nature, coupled with complex injuries and medications, stifled further deliberations in my mind. I didn't question if this was the best course of action but calmly accepted the news. "This is what we need to do," I agreed. My focus centered on the timing of Barry's entrance into heaven: Palm Sunday or Easter?

Sharon, broken with grief, cried so hard she hyperventilated, causing her hands to grow numb. She crawled into bed with me, curled up in a fetal position, and sobbed. She recalls, "It was the worst day of my life." We all felt the weight ... a family in crisis, crushed by a sense of hopelessness.

But one quiet question transformed our situation. A point of view I hadn't considered. "Are you sure? Are you *sure* you want to do this so soon?"

One voice changed my responses forever. My mom's. Her words nudged me to gather more input. I placed two calls outside our immediate circle: one to our pastor and one to the president of the college that employed my husband. I had accepted Barry's imminent death because I thought I had to. But I gained a new perspective after listening to the men's support of keeping Barry on the respirator. "There's no hurry," they both said in separate conversations. "People around the world are praying. Let's see what God will do."

When Jana heard of my deliberations, she raced from Altoona to Johnstown. Her only conversation had been with the surgeon whose counsel favored a wait-and-see approach. By the time she arrived, I had just hung up the phone. We agreed. We would wait.

Pull the plug? By faith, my final answer only could be a prayerful "No!"

As one day slipped into another, we continued to be surrounded and overwhelmed by setbacks and uncertainty. I felt haunted by the if onlys and what ifs. Being encircled by so many differing opinions felt confusing. I didn't find it easy to read God's direction but could only hope I'd made the right decision.

Difficulties often present seemingly impossible choices. Who knows what to do when perspectives contradict and counsel differs? While processing our journey, I recalled a parallel story in John 11 that helped me work through my own. An account of illness, death, multiple points of view ... and a divine perspective that made all the difference.

If Only ...

Their shoulders slumped as they knelt over the still form of their brother. It was too late. Just that morning, Mary and Martha had sent word to Jesus, telling Him of their brother's illness. Of his imminent death. Had their message even reached Him?

How could this have happened? If only Jesus had been there …

Duty brought the sisters to their feet. They must prepare the body for burial. The death wail announced the passing of Lazarus. Neighbors and friends gathered to comfort the family. Within a matter of hours, they placed the body, carefully wrapped in linen, in a nearby cave.

If only …

The day of death passed. If only … Another day went by. If only … Then another. Where was Jesus? Finally, on the fourth day, He came. Martha addressed Him with regret, Lord, "if you had been here, my brother would not have died."[2]

Those who came to support the sisters whispered, "Could not he who opened the eyes of the blind man have kept this man from dying?"[3]

The faith of the sisters and their friends stood out to me. They truly expected and believed Jesus could have healed Lazarus. They sent a message to Him. They knew without a doubt He could have helped.

When I read this, I identified with Martha. Like her, I tried to exercise my faith, ask for God's help, and make the right decision. Yet Barry's brain injury made his condition more and more uncertain. I felt helpless and found myself burying my hopes and dreams. I mourned the absence of what could have been.

If only the late morning fog hadn't occurred …
If only the doctors hadn't induced the coma …
If only Barry would wake up …

What If …

Four days later, Jesus decided to go back to Judea. His disciples likely shook their heads, apprehension and fear evident in their eyes. Increased hostility of the religious leaders toward Jesus and His piercing message put His safety in jeopardy. Hadn't they all just hurried to safety nearly a day's journey away? Mary and Martha didn't actually ask Jesus to come. And the people here expressed receptivity to Him. Now Jesus wanted to go back? What ifs consumed them.

When the disciples understood the gravity of the condition of Lazarus and Jesus' intent, their reactions ricocheted from a practical "But Rabbi" to resigning themselves to a deadly fate.

Following Jesus. No matter how noble the intent, what ifs often flood our minds and hold us back. As with the disciples, these what ifs can move far beyond caution. They symbolize our fears, rooted in thoughts about things that are not real ... a guess about the future.[4]

In the aftermath of the crash, as we began our long journey of recovery, I bumped into what-if questions around every corner.

What if Barry never wakes up?

What if brain damage leaves him severely disabled?

What if he never comes home?

What if he needs special care?

What if I have to make this terrifying decision again?

What if I find myself a widow ... and a single mom?

Over and over, I had to rein in my speculations and focus on truth. I had to leave my if onlys and what ifs with the One who holds the world in His hands. Worry could not change the past or alter the future. I clung to verses such as Deuteronomy 33:27: "The eternal God is your refuge, and underneath are the everlasting arms." With God's help, I hoped I could consistently choose to trust Him with our future through all the todays and every tomorrow.

Cautious Optimism

Weeks passed with only subtle changes in Barry's condition. His brainstem still exhibited excessive swelling, and bleeding from the brain needed to be reabsorbed. The medical staff experimented with a cocktail of drugs that had successfully helped other people revive after head injuries. They also moved Barry out of ICU and gradually weaned him off the respirator. Just seventeen days after his initial injuries, he breathed on his own with only the aid of oxygen. He began to move his limbs to a limited degree. And although his comatose condition remained very serious, his doctors used terms like "cautiously optimistic."

When I could finally visit him, I apologized to his still form. "I know you always said you didn't want to be kept alive like this, but we need you. Please come back to us!"

At that moment, someone in blue scrubs stepped into the room. I sought yet another point of view. "How long before we need to grapple with the hard ethical questions?"

He paused and looked down at me in my wheelchair and halo, then spoke softly. "I'd say a year."

I nodded and took a deep breath. Okay. We'd do a year.

Due to the severity of his injuries, Barry's immunity registered extremely low. The medical personnel discovered pneumonia and a kidney infection. Heavy doses of antibiotics dripped through his IV. He could not leave the hospital until these complications resolved themselves. More major challenges in an already delicate situation.

We didn't know until later about the prayer meetings taking place ... people pleading for Barry's life. Again, unseen pictures of light surrounded us when we needed them most.

I could never have envisioned our family facing a deadly dilemma like this. In the midst of so many points of view, along with the if onlys and what ifs, I had to trust that God superintended my final decision. His omniscient point of view, as He penned our story, represented a perspective much broader than we ever could have imagined.

CHAPTER SIX

A Surprising Point of View

Earth's crammed with heaven,
And every common bush afire with God;
But only he who sees takes off his shoes;
The rest sit round it and pluck blackberries.[1]
~ Elizabeth Barrett Browning

I LONGED TO experience God's presence in hospital hallways, surrounded by difficult diagnoses. I wanted to see a reason to take off my shoes as Moses did in the wilderness when he encountered the burning bush. In the middle of differing opinions, I needed a divine point of view.

In the craft of writing, point of view (POV) communicates who tells the story which, in turn, influences how it is told.

When authors use first person POV, they use *I* or *we*. It's close and conversational, lending itself to personal experience stories or memoirs. But it limits the reader to one perspective.

Third person POV uses *he, she, it,* and *they*. There are basically two types. (Hang with me here.) In third person limited, the narrator brings you the story through one or two character's eyes, but he doesn't know all.

In third person omniscient, there's an all-knowing and all-seeing narrator who allows the reader into the thoughts of all the characters.

We, as humans, naturally see the world in first person from our limited viewpoint. God, on the other hand, has an omniscient point of view. He's the all-knowing, all-seeing writer of perfect stories, concerned with what's best for all His characters. He longs to share His perspective with us, to broaden our view and help us see beyond the first-person-tangible to the eternal. To surprise us with a glimpse of something more.

God's Point of View

As the omniscient, all-knowing narrator, God uses His knowledge to pierce through outward appearances into the very heart of each of us. His point of view has no limits.

I find comfort in the fact that God demonstrates a divine seeing, hearing, and knowing far beyond anything we could ever imagine or replicate. In contrast to our superficial vision, His eyes "range throughout the earth to strengthen those whose hearts are fully committed to him."[2] Solomon, the wise king of Israel wrote, "For a man's ways are in full view of the LORD, and he examines *all* his paths. ... The eyes of the Lord are *everywhere,* ..."[3]

When God writes our life stories, He sees every event, every behavior, and every attitude. As the ultimate multi-tasker, His omniscient POV trumps our limited, first person, temporal perspective of our lives, our relationships, and our circumstances.

God sees what mere men miss.

God's omniscient POV became personal to me when I realized He saw deep into the layers of our trauma. He monitored the obstacles that plagued us and prevented us from fulfilling even the simplest of responsibilities. With clarity and compassion, He witnessed our pain, our frustrations, our complications, our I-don't-know-what-to-do moments, and our nagging fears as we faced an uncertain future.

I'm still learning that God's POV enables Him to write our life stories with infinite wisdom and grace. He fits our paragraphs together with all-knowing eyes and all-powerful hands as the ever-present Father we can trust—no matter what.

Take Away the Stone

When I compared the human perspectives in the Lazarus story—Mary, Martha, the Jewish mourners, and the disciples—with Jesus' omniscient POV, I found a startling difference. His take on their story included so much more than what they could see. He shared His position with the disciples: "This sickness will not end in death. No, it is for God's glory so that God's Son may be glorified through it. ... so that you may believe."[4]

To Martha, He asked, "Did I not tell you that if you believed, you would see the glory of God?"[5] Even in His prayer to His Father, He reiterated His divine and eternal purpose: "... that they may believe that you sent me."[6]

Four days passed. Enough time to eliminate any question of the reality of Lazarus's death. Enough time for the community to feel the loss. Enough time to begin the grieving process.

Jesus, approaching the grave—and clearly in charge of the situation—instructed them in no uncertain terms, "Take away the stone."

The mournful chatter fell away. Every eye, full of questions, stared at Jesus. Practical Martha questioned the wisdom of opening a grave after four days. Finally, a few men stepped forward, broke the seal, and heaved the stone aside to reveal the cave entrance. The crowd held its collective breath.

"Jesus called in a loud voice, 'Lazarus, come out!' The dead man came out, his hands and feet wrapped with strips of linen, and a cloth around his face. Jesus said to them, 'Take off the grave clothes and let him go.'"[7]

Imagine being there. Hear the deafening silence as the crowd, frozen in time, waits to see what will happen. See their eyes open wider and wider as a four-day-dead mummy shuffles out of the tomb. Join the ensuing chaos as the sisters of Lazarus rush to unwind the burial linen from their beloved brother. As tears flow and cries of joy echo off the walls of the burial cave, notice Lazarus searching the crowd until his eyes lock with those of Jesus, his friend.

And help yourself to the feast Martha likely pulls together to celebrate the occasion. Had a funeral, four days past, ever morphed into a commemoration of life before?

To Him Be Glory

"Therefore many of the Jews who had come to visit Mary, and had seen what Jesus did, put their faith in him."[8]

The people in this story did what they knew. They sent a message to Jesus relaying the news of Lazarus's illness. Per His instructions, they took away the stone. Even their faith in Jesus' ability to heal had somewhat predictable outcomes. They expected Him to do what He had done in the past. The disciples only saw calamity ahead.

Yet, all along, Jesus possessed a higher and broader perspective, an omniscient point of view each character could never have imagined. In the midst of their unmet expectations, they found themselves completely surprised by something more. Something new. Even Lazarus. Perhaps rubbing shoulders with the demonstration of this resurrection prepared them for Jesus' greater resurrection a short time later.

Transitions

Jesus knew from the beginning that He would raise Lazarus from the dead. In *our* story, what parts of it did He anticipate that our human eyes could not yet see?

It took twelve days for Barry's pneumonia to clear up. Transfer to the Mountain View Care Center was imminent, and I would be going home. But even as we moved ahead, I knew we had a long road ahead of us. The older girls cried together over the projection that their dad would likely be disabled to a significant degree.

The college president named an interim academic dean to fill in for Barry. In an email dated May 5, 2003, he wrote, "Because of the pressing nature of many aspects of Barry's role, I have determined that we need someone to lead that area of the school, knowing that if and when Barry returns to health, we will welcome him back and have him leading the academic area once again." I appreciated the president's optimism, loyalty—and faith. Yet I quietly wondered if Barry would ever be able to work again.

Jana later wrote about her feelings at the time of Barry's transition:

I spent six weeks with my father in Altoona. He was unconscious that entire time. I talked with him every day, I played music for him, I held his hand, talked some more, wished and hoped and prayed for a miracle, wondered if we were doing the right thing because I knew he would have hated being on all those machines. I did everything I could.

I remember the night I said goodbye and let go of being there every second. I couldn't be with my mom *and* ride in the ambulance with my dad *and* drive my car back all at the same time. Several minutes after I left, Aunt Karen came into the room. Dad opened his eyes and asked for "Jana."

In Karen's words, Barry began to move, and as if in slow motion, repeated the same word over and over. Finally, she could make out the name, "Jaaannnaaa."

The next morning, the ambulance pulled around to the hospital doors. "Barry," the EMT greeted the tall, thin frame on the gurney, "we're taking you to Clarks Summit."

The ears, which for thirty-three days appeared deaf, heard. His lips, which had only whispered Jana's name hours before, spoke. "That's home," he said.

Beyond Our Expectations

Through the following weeks and months, Barry climbed out of the coma, bit by bit. The physician who made rounds at the nursing home placed a feeding tube to enable my pale, too-thin husband to finally receive regular nourishment. As Barry's condition improved, he became more and more agitated. He fell out of bed, repeatedly yanked out his trach, and needed constant supervision. He exhibited confusion. His swallowing challenges necessitated thick liquids. The girls and I felt disheartened. Based on the Rancho Scale,[9] a tool used to describe levels of brain function, the staff reassured us this was all part of the recovery process.

Gradually, Barry became more aware of his surroundings. One day, the supervisor called in tears. "He's singing with the tape!" The girls and I had recorded our voices with loving messages, Scripture, and hymns. He began to recognize us when we came to visit. Physical therapists patiently worked to restore his strength and balance. In time, speech therapists offered exercises and even games to sharpen his mind.

Eight long weeks after my agonizing decision to keep him on the breathing machine, I again explained to Barry what had happened to our family. This time he understood, reached for my hand—and wept.

From my viewpoint, we were given no human reason to hope my husband would recover, even to this level. But God could not be bound by our predictable, limited expectations. He was writing Barry's story from an omniscient point of view with a plot incorporating immeasurably more than all we could ask or imagine.[10]

God invites us to tell Him about our circumstances: "Lord, the one you love is sick." He may give us simple and, perhaps, counterintuitive, directions: "Take away the stone." But in the end, we may have the joy of unwrapping His blessings four days, four years, even forty years later. He broadens our view and surprises us with something more.

Barry's injuries did not end in death. No, it was for God's glory so that God's Son would be glorified through it.[11]

Your Story

God alone possesses an all-seeing, all-knowing point of view. Consider a loss or unmet expectation you've experienced in spite of your best efforts. Compare your if onlys and what ifs with how God views your situation according to Scripture. Describe a time when your first person viewpoint discouraged you from trusting God's all-encompassing perspective. Meditate on what you've learned in chapters five and six about God's omniscience and His ability to see and do more than we ask or think. Write a prayer or a story of trust. Refer to Psalm 139:1-12; John 11; and Ephesians 3:20.

CHAPTER SEVEN

Snapshots That Surrounded Us

THE PICTURES OF our story brightened as the dark questions of our survival receded into the background. Yet I struggled to trust God with the effects our injuries had on the people around us.

Trauma and suffering extended far beyond Barry and me on that fateful day in early April. As time went on, family and friends shared how our story affected them. I hung on to every word. And as I pieced together *their* pictures, the layers of *our* story became clearer. Over and over I wrestled with the reality of their suffering, their losses. I found myself feeling sorry, even guilty, for what they experienced. Could I entrust those closest to us into His care?

Jana

Every weekend, Jana drove the two-hour winding route home from college to work a catering job. She happened to be home on the day of the crash when the call came. An Altoona Hospital chaplain kindly explained to her that there had been a car accident and her dad was in critical condition undergoing emergency surgery. At that point, no one could be sure he would pull through. The whereabouts of her mom and sisters? The chaplain had no idea.

Shortly after, my dad and mom called her with news about the girls and me. As the day wore on, they pieced together that Sharon and I had been taken to Johnstown, Elisabeth to Pittsburgh. By late afternoon, Jana caravanned with my parents to try to find us and sort out what was going on.

On the five-hour trip to Johnstown, she called and chatted

with her little sister in Pittsburgh and conferred with Barry's nurse in Altoona. After a somber visit to see Sharon and me, Pastor Frank, who had met them in Johnstown, drove Jana to Altoona to see her dad. In the darkness of that night, she found him swollen and unconscious, hooked up to a multitude of tubes and machines.

Jana had a unique relationship with Barry. Of the two of us, he was always the one who understood her best. She later wrote, "I will never forget the security I felt during my first two years of college—my dad let go of me and believed I would succeed. This is one of the greatest gifts I've ever been given."

After the crash, her attitude was, "If I don't protect my father, who is in such a vulnerable state, then who will?" This became the driving force that stayed with Jana through the early stages of Barry's recovery. By recommendation of his team of doctors, who recognized his critical and fragile condition, she requested no visitors. Besides, she needed space to manage it all. Nevertheless, his friends and colleagues filled the waiting room and inundated the nurses' station with phone calls, asking to see him. I'm sure they wanted to show their support. But to a college girl who could lose her dad at any time, she felt overrun. To Jana, it seemed no one listened to or respected her request. She felt relieved when Pastor Frank offered to be the point of contact with our community.

I couldn't be with her or with Barry during those critical early hours. I could do nothing to help. Yet, looking back, I have to trust that a guiding unseen Presence surrounded them both.

Sharon

Sharon's name became the first thought in my groggy mind. Slowly, bits and pieces of the crash scene began to fit together like puzzle pieces in my memory. A pressing urgency to see her gripped me. As the driver, she could *not* bear the blame for all that happened to us. I knew. I had coached her in the fatal fog.

Sharon. Our mellow middle child—quiet, unassuming, compassionate. A good student, she also played soccer, took piano lessons, and participated in the church youth group.

Besides a concussion, Sharon suffered a minor ankle injury. The staff never did find her school jacket or her new sneakers and jeans.

When she tiptoed into my room, my maternal eyes surveyed her fragile frame and pale appearance. I longed to hold her close and tell her everything would be fine. But I could only try to reassure her. "This was *not* your fault, hon," I whispered. "You did the best you could. There was nothing else you could've done. All we can do now is entrust it all to God."

She nodded weakly, tears in her eyes.

Several times over the next few weeks, Sharon visited Barry. The two of them had enjoyed a relationship all their own. As an athlete, she liked to hike with him, ride bikes, play ball, and garden. She loved their breakfast and lunch dates. What thoughts ran through her mind as she held his hand, asked God to heal him, and tried to coax him out of his coma?

I could only imagine Sharon's anguish and fear. I didn't want this tragedy to cast a dark shadow on the way she viewed herself or her future. Over days and weeks, I begged God to wrap her in His warm, supernatural grace.

Elisabeth

I cannot remember when they took Elisabeth from my side. After some preliminary tests, the EMT wheeled her to a helicopter headed for Pittsburgh Children's Hospital (PCH). Unlike the rest of us, she remembers her once-in-a-lifetime ride.

"Where are we?" she asked the nurse as she sat next to the pilot, gazing out the window in her miniature neck brace. "What's that whiteness?"

"The clouds," he told her, keeping a close eye on his patient. "Are you okay?"

Time would tell her true condition. But for the moment, she seemed fine.

Elisabeth's concussion resulted in two black eyes. Her car seat cracked in the crash but did its job well.

That evening, our five-year-old—who just that morning had witnessed the fiery nightmare of a twenty-three car pile-up— fell asleep before she could eat her supper.

Elisabeth recalls lots of stickers inside the CT scan machine, yummy pancakes for breakfast the next morning, and the nurse taking her to the hospital library in a red wagon. Her roommate's family brought balloons to the little girl whose parents lay miles away in critical condition.

Our youngest daughter noticed her roommate had visitors, but no one came to see her. The staff reassured her that someone would come soon. Grammy and Poppy finally arrived after their initial visit to see Sharon and me.

"Were you afraid?" Grammy asked.

"No," she said with certainty. "God was with me."

For Elisabeth to be discharged, they needed a car seat, which the hospital loaned them. Weeks later, after we returned home, my dad and I shopped for the safest replacement we could find, thankful to have one to use in the meantime.

With Elisabeth's release, our family had two people in critical condition in two locations fifty miles apart and a bouncy five-year-old to look after at the guesthouse near my hospital. Jana purchased a few outfits so Elisabeth had something to wear. Pastor Frank brought some toys and gifts from friends back home. During the weeks to come, Barry's sister-in-law, Karen, read stories, played games, did crafts, and made sure our little girl rested—doctor's orders.

While still hospitalized, I received a postcard from the EMT who made the decision to life-flight Elisabeth to PCH. She shared her concern and asked about Elisabeth's condition. I tearfully hugged the letter to my heart. Afterward, we chatted on the phone, and I expressed my deepest appreciation.

Later, when my parents drove me back to the Johnstown hospital to have my halo removed, my mom shared, "This is the elevator Elisabeth loved to ride—up and down, up and down." Seeing the transparent glass, I could just picture her, grinning and chattering away. "We ate our meals here," Mom mentioned as we ate lunch in the cafeteria before driving home. "Elisabeth had meatloaf and mashed potatoes as often as she could." Yep. Always the meat and potato girl, to this day.

Our late-in-life baby, with sisters eleven and fourteen years older, brought us all joy. She breathed fun ... and sensitivity. She loved reading and playing games with her daddy. And she enjoyed preschool, one of the few experiences that stayed the same that spring.

Elisabeth's simple faith in the presence of God helped me entrust her to His keeping. Because of our limitations, her life would likely be different from that of her older sisters. I clung to the truth that the God of the universe would go with her ... and with us all.

I missed a significant chapter of our girls' lives in the five weeks after the crash. I would never recover this segment of time, but I wanted to know and understand everything they experienced and felt. Everything.

Barb

On a continent south of the equator, three weeks after the crash, my sister thumbed through hard copies of the last several weeks' worth of email. As missionaries in the bush of Tanzania, East Africa, Brad and Barb traveled only occasionally to the nearest town for supplies, mail, and email. At that time, no cell phone or Internet towers dotted the Serengeti. Communication with family was sporadic at best. As Barb read the emails at her kitchen table, most recent news first, she found disturbing references to my surgery and the uncertainty of Barry's life. Nothing made sense. Finally, she began to read from the beginning, email after email. The shock of her only sibling's condition and the precarious nature of her brother-in-law's health felt overwhelming. She later said, "It was like a dream, a horrible nightmare."

Brad's trip into town happened to be the day before they drove their children ten hours back to boarding school in Nairobi, Kenya. When they arrived in Nairobi, my sister called our parents who had been trying to reach her since their first hospital visit in Johnstown. "Should I come home?" she asked. My mom said no because of the long distance. They talked several more times.

Barb also called me at HealthSouth in Altoona. I couldn't believe it. We cried together, two sisters on two continents, bonded together, miles notwithstanding.

Sensing the distress of my parents, Brad again phoned them to ask if Barb should come home. This time, Mom admitted, "It would be nice." Two days later, Barb flew from Nairobi to Newark. She told me later she couldn't help but think, *I could be going home to a funeral.*

Dad and Mom

I could see it in my parents' eyes. The strain, the stress, the worry.

After they received the initial call from the scene, a state trooper called them, but their phone malfunctioned. They could hear him, but he could not hear them, so he hung up. Frustration escalated as they prepared to face a situation for which no one can be prepared. They followed a friend from Johnstown to Pittsburgh to pick up Elisabeth. The friend made sure they didn't get lost in an unfamiliar city.

After Elisabeth's discharge, Dad and Mom stayed in Johnstown with me. They listened as surgeons explained risks and procedures. They prayed in the OR waiting room through two long operations. They soothed me in the ICU when I became agitated. They pushed the morphine button when the pain made me forget. They fed me when I could finally swallow. As the days wore on, they hung with me. They nurtured Sharon and Elisabeth. When I transferred to a rehab facility in Altoona, they brought the two girls to their home.

I can't imagine my hospital stay without them. They supported me in every way possible. But exhaustion and stress took its toll. My sister came home—for my sake, yes, but for their benefit as well. Looking back, I thank God for Barb's listening ear, her support, and her care for them. Our family needed to be together in the aftermath of this crisis, a crisis with repercussions that would not be resolved for a long, long time.

Barry's Family

Barry's siblings, Maxine and Gary, drove to Altoona, leaving their ninety-year-old father in Michigan. The news of Barry's condition greatly upset Dad Phillips. He stayed with Maxine's husband, Ernie, for a time while, day after day, Maxine and Gary faithfully hovered by Barry's side in Altoona, along with Rayan, Maxine's daughter, who also supported Jana in multiple ways. Later, Peter, Rayan's fiancé, drove to Pennsylvania to lend his support. Karen, Gary's wife, offered invaluable help in Johnstown. On some days, various ones traveled the fifty miles back and forth between Barry's hospital and mine. They lost valuable work hours at home, not to mention sharing in the strain of it all.

Picture after picture demonstrated the all-encompassing nature of our trauma: Jana's management of the crisis, Sharon's struggle with guilt, little Elisabeth's all-alone trauma, my sister's lengthy, uncertain flight, my parents' stress, Barry's family's long days of waiting, hoping, and praying for a miracle. It all made me feel sad and guilty as I tried to put myself in their shoes. I pieced their perspectives together but could do little to change the emerging picture. Would I trust the perfect, purposeful, omniscient God with their stories too?

CHAPTER EIGHT

Will You Trust Me?

As I write our story now, I see it differently than when I experienced it in the moment. As months and years move us farther away from the scene, I perceive a perspective much broader than I did when wheeling my way into Barry's hospital room in my halo or counting laps using my walker in rehab. Not that I fully understand why the turnpike collision occurred or realize an untold number of benefits. I don't. But I have learned some unforgettable truths about myself, about people ... and about God.

A storyteller or an author who writes stories creates a central character or protagonist and, through the ups and downs of the plot, develops him. The character changes, grows, conquers, and brings resolution. Often, this process involves outer and inner conflict, difficult decisions, or even life-threatening events—all to bring the character to the point of transformation. But if no growth occurs, the story feels flat, disappointing. It fails to bring inspiration to the reader.

God, as the Master Writer, crafts our stories with a plot that develops us and builds character into our lives from the inside out. Just as an author shapes his characters, God desires to help us grow. He equips us "with everything good for doing his will," and works in us "what is pleasing to him, through Jesus Christ, ..."[1] With the love only a heavenly Father can offer, He draws us to Himself. He invites us to trust Him.

As I've processed our story, I have to believe our trauma was not an accident. Could I continue to trust God with His providence? Can *we* trust God enough to follow, even when we can't see where He is taking us? Will we align our conflicted feelings with the truth of His Word? Will we embrace the opportunity to grow and change even when it means pain and uncertainty?

Growing in the Desert

On a typical Sunday morning in March 2003, a month before the crash, I claimed my usual seat at church, sang my usual alto, and took notes on what the pastor shared. Based on James 1:2-4, he titled his message, "How to Be Ready for Anything." The last sentence I jotted down read, *See your trials as God's best plan.* Although I listened with an open heart, I sat unsuspecting and oblivious to what God would allow our family to experience just a few short weeks later.

James, the half-brother of Jesus, wrote the first words of the New Testament to believers in Christ who had been forced from their homes because of persecution. "Consider it wholly joyful," James encouraged them, "whenever you are enveloped in *or* encounter trials of any sort *or* fall into various temptations. Be assured *and* understand that the trial *and* proving of your faith bring out endurance *and* steadfastness *and* patience."[2]

Usually, we associate growth with ideal conditions. Plants thrive in rich, moist soil, in a greenhouse-like environment. But James links "trials of any sort" with the growth points of endurance, steadfastness, and patience.

Trials and trauma remind me more of a desert than a greenhouse. A dry, thirsty, barren place of wandering, of loneliness and discouragement. Because of the accident, I had to accept that God's way of developing us often includes the wilderness, the place where the fruits of spiritual growth and inner strength grow best. Perhaps, as a result of our circumstances, God would make us more sensitive and more effective in our relationships and in our service.

Robert J. Morgan in his book, *The Red Sea Rules*, offers a helpful perspective. He writes:

> We don't always know why God allows problems, but we know He intends to use them to heighten our maturity and deepen our faith. Trials and troubles are dumbbells and treadmills for the soul. They develop strength and stamina.[3]

The apostle Paul penned a parallel thought: "We also rejoice in our sufferings, because we know that suffering produces perseverance; perseverance, character; and character, hope."[4]

Hope. In the throes of my many questions, I needed hope.

Hope grows out of trust, which includes reliance on God, confidence in His Word, dependence on His perfect ways, and faith in the all-seeing God who has a reason for everything He allows. Hope grows out of our belief that as God writes our stories, He develops our character.

Over the weeks and months of my recovery, God graciously showed me His faithful care and flawless attributes. Little by little, I understood and appreciated His trustworthiness. Familiar truths became deeply personal like they were intended just for me. My dialogues with God became increasingly meaningful as He quieted my mind with His Word. I still treasure those simple, broken conversations in the quiet of the night. While still wearing my neck brace, I wrote these dialogues with God in the form of a story.

Will You Trust Me? An Allegory

In the fullness of time, there lived a just and loving King. Although no walls surrounded His kingdom, a single gate graced a quiet hillside with a wooden cross situated nearby. To become a true citizen of the kingdom, one had only to kneel by the cross, thereby acknowledging the King's mercy and accepting the new name given to those who turn from their dark ways and follow His light.

At the age of six, a young girl knelt before the cross with a desire to serve the good King with all her heart. As she grew up, she sought to please Him in all of her choices. Later, she and her husband served together in the kingdom of light.

In time, children were born. The couple often took them on walks near the gate and wooden cross and read to them from the King's Book. They wanted the children to know the loving King, and they prayed that the enticing words of darkness would not lure them away.

On a certain day in the spring of the year, as the servants journeyed through the land, a confusing fog dropped in front of them like a curtain. Without sight of the way, they stumbled and veered off the path to plummet down, down to the bottom of a rocky ravine. Here they lay, bleeding and broken.

The King's gaze penetrated the dense whiteness. He sent angels at just the right time to help His servants in their time of need (Psalm 91:11). He loved them with an everlasting love (Jeremiah 31:3). Though this trial of their faith would bring many questions and fears, He knew, in the end, their service to Him would come forth as gold (Job 23:10) and bring honor to His name (1 Peter 1:7).

Not long after the fateful plunge off the cliff, the woman lay in bed unable to move. "Oh, King, they tell me my husband is dying in a faraway place. His caregivers shake their heads with whispered uncertainty. What is this twisted widowhood I feel?"

He answered, "Do not fear, for I am with you; do not be dismayed, for I am your God. I will strengthen you and help you; I will uphold you with my righteous right hand" (Isaiah 41:10).

And the peace of God, which transcends all understanding, kept guard of her heart and mind (Philippians 4:7). One of her helpers asked, "How can you be so strong?"

"Strong? Oh, Lord, I feel so weak. And these screws that bore into my head ... I cannot move. I can no longer even look from side to side."

The King took her hand and said, "My child, this will do more than help your body heal. Your heart will be reminded to look only to Me, the author and perfecter of your faith (Hebrews 12:2). As for the screws, remember the crown of thorns I bore for you. You, too, can wear these for the glory of My kingdom."

And the woman replied, "Oh, my Lord, I will try to live one day at a time because Your compassions never fail. They are new every morning; great is Your faithfulness" (Lamentations 3:22, 23).

Then she whispered, "Your Majesty, my children. They weep because they are afraid. They grieve the loss of what was before."

His voice grew soft and tender. "I did not allow this to happen to you without knowing fully how it would affect those around you. I have promised that all things work together for good, not only in your life but for them also (Romans 8:28). My ways are not your ways (Isaiah 55:8, 9). Trust Me, My daughter. I am an ever-present help in trouble (Psalm 46:1). Lean hard.

Both you and your children are secure in My everlasting arms" (Deuteronomy 33:27).

And with tears in her eyes, she prayed that her weakness would strengthen her children's faith, and they would better trust the only parent without limitations, the King Himself.

"Oh, Sir, we have so many needs," she said. "They knock on my door asking for payment. We cannot work or even walk as we once did."

"I will teach you another one of My names," the kind ruler answered. "It is Jehovah-Jireh. I have foreseen all your needs and will provide according to My great riches (Philippians 4:19). Trust Me to make all grace abound toward you. You will have all you need for each day (2 Corinthians 9:8). I will also send My other servants to share with you. Their sacrifice pleases Me (Hebrews 13:16), so welcome it graciously. There will come a day when you will serve Me better because you have had to receive."

And she began to record all the ways Jehovah-Jireh kept His promises in ways far more than all she could ask or imagine (Ephesians 3:20).

"Oh, dear God, why? Did we disappoint You? Weren't we faithful enough? Perhaps some sin lay hidden in our hearts? And what about the future? I'm afraid to go out, to travel again, afraid of the fog, the rain, afraid of ... the unknown. What if ... Could You ... would You set a rainbow over our heads, a promise that we will always be safe and well?"

After a time He slowly answered:

I have redeemed you; I have summoned you by name; you are mine (Isaiah 43:1). Am I not permitted to do what I choose with what is mine (Matthew 20:15 AMPC)? Does not the potter have the right to make out of the same lump of clay some pottery for noble purposes and some for common use (Romans 9:21)? Does the clay say to the potter, "What are you making (Isaiah 45:9)?"

You speak of rainbows. Consider this: When you pass through the waters, I will be with you; and when you pass through the rivers, they will not sweep over you. When you walk through the fire, you will not be burned; … (Isaiah 43:2).

Will you trust Me?

Thoughtfully, I made my way again to the gate on the hillside. With a willing heart, I knelt down … and placed a white rose of surrender at the foot of the cross.

Your Story

God, as the Master Writer, is crafting your story with a plot that will develop you and build character into your life from the inside out. From chapter seven, consider God's providence in light of the stories/experiences of others that may cause *you* to feel pain and guilt. From chapter eight, reflect on your desert-like trials and how they bring the potential for personal and spiritual development. Which questions and answers in the allegory resonate with your story? Why is surrender an integral part of trusting God? Meditate on what you've learned in chapters seven and eight about God's personal involvement in your growth. Write a prayer or a story of trust. Refer to James 1:2, 3 and Romans 5:3, 4.

PART TWO

IN THE BEGINNING . . .
SEPTEMBER 12, 1958 - APRIL 5, 2003

CHAPTER NINE

The Story Behind the Story

WHERE DO YOU go on vacation with a seventeen-year-old and a preschooler? We chose the Pittsburgh Zoo. Maps and travel brochures littered our kitchen table as we planned our trip. Less than a five-hour drive from Scranton, it seemed feasible for a long weekend.

On Thursday, April 3, 2003, the four of us said goodbye to Jana, home from college to work for the weekend. We buckled up and wound our way through the Pennsylvania mountains. A motel room with an efficiency unit became our temporary home as we ventured to visit the zoo, the Carnegie Museum, and the National Aviary. On Friday night, while Elisabeth slept and I journaled, Barry and Sharon enjoyed a daddy-daughter date to the Duquesne Incline to see the city lights. We planned our return trip to include a quick stop in Hershey on Saturday morning. Only God knew of our impending detour.

What's behind the story of a family returning from vacation one minute and facing an overwhelming calamity the next?

Growing Up

Buffalo blizzards. Buffalo Bills football. Buffalo wings.

Born a Buffalo baby in 1958, I grew up in the suburb of West Seneca, New York, named after long-forgotten Native Americans and situated ten minutes from downtown. Our family took frequent trips to the breezy Buffalo Marina, which offered big ice cream cones for a small price. Every summer, we crossed the Peace Bridge into Fort Erie, Ontario, and meandered up the Niagara Parkway to see The Falls where, every second, over 3,000 tons of water thunder over and down into the swirling whirlpools below. We took daring Maid-of-the-Mist voyages and quiet strolls amidst a plethora of colorful blooms in the many manicured gardens nearby.

Twenty miles to the east of us, my grandparents, aunts, uncles, and cousins made every spaghetti dinner and picnic a special event that fed a feeling of belonging and stirred an appreciation for my heritage. I pulled my chair closer to hear about the olden days. My courageous great-grandparents crossed the Atlantic to find religious freedom and a better life in America and Canada. In the old barn behind the house, my paternal grandfather, an artist and musician, painted trays of souvenirs for the shops in Niagara Falls.

Dad worked for the gas company, and Mom left her nursing career to stay home with Barb and me. We rough-housed with Dad and learned homemaking—and math facts—with Mom. Our vacations, though frugal, took us to Boston, Washington, D.C., and Philadelphia. As part of our church youth group, we tubed down snow-covered hills in winter, counted the days until camp in the Adirondack Mountains every summer, and participated in service projects year round. My parents not only took us to church but consistently modeled their biblical beliefs.

Crooked

Born with clubbed feet, I wore what my parents called "special shoes." These were infant shoes that looked like I had them on the wrong feet. "They did the trick," Mom liked to say as she remembered them. Over three years of orthodontic work did the trick to correct a significant overbite. As a teen, I developed scoliosis. The exercises didn't help much, but I didn't worry about it then. Years later, my surgeons had to work around the spinal curvature they said would worsen with age.

Love and Marriage

Within my first few weeks on our college campus in 1975, I met Barry. His family farmed thirteen acres of Concord grapes near Kalamazoo, Michigan. Along with tying, trimming, and harvesting grapes, Dad Phillips did carpentry work. Gary inherited his skills, but Barry liked books. Even as a young boy, he habitually got up at 5:00 a.m. to read until the bus came for school.

Barry liked to tell our daughters about the list of girls' names and phone numbers he once carried in his pocket. When a college event warranted a date, he called the first name on the list. If he couldn't get through or the girl said no, he called the second name, and on it went. Somehow, Sarah Ewert made the list. On our first date, he took me to the campus fall play. My name moved up the list as time went by, and soon the others disappeared. I found flowers and notes in my mailbox, an escort home from the library every evening, and stacks of letters from him the following summer. We became engaged just before my junior year. While waiting for me to finish college, he picked up a master's degree to add to his two bachelor's degrees, and we finally married on July 14, 1979.

Hand in Hand

Barry's first job as a junior high history teacher brought us to a suburb of Rochester, New York. I spent some of my happiest days keeping house in our little subsidized apartment and assisting in the church and school. After studying for his doctorate during the next three summers, Barry became the school principal.

Three and a half years after we married, Jana arrived, and Sharon became her little sister nearly three years later. Our love for our daughters fueled a desire to play with them, read stories, train, and teach them. After we tucked them into bed, we spent the evenings remodeling our first home. When God opened the door for Barry to teach at a Christian college in Northeast Pennsylvania in 1987, the house sold with the first showing. We regretted leaving our friends and ministry in New York after eight years, but we felt eager for the opportunity to impact and mentor students.

Barry taught education courses and supervised student teachers at the college. After several years, he spearheaded the process of teacher certification with the State Education Department while maintaining Middle States accreditation. He also laid the foundation for the graduate school. When the school reorganized in 1993, he assumed the role of Vice President for College Academics.

Barry's Type A personality and drive meant busy days, often brainstorming at 3:00 a.m. It meant making lists during Sunday sermons. He seemed self-sufficient and readily foresaw the implications of policies and decisions. A multiplicity of ideas sent him in many directions at once. At the same time, his love for books and study never diminished. He earned two more master's degrees and another doctorate from the seminary associated with the college. At home, he handled our finances, gave direction when decisions had to be made, and generally led the way for the family.

But Barry didn't always carry a book or file folder. He made time for our daughters, interacting with them about school and teaching them strategy through games. He often made paper route deals with them: "I'll deliver your newspapers on Saturday morning if you'll sleep in." Or, "I'll buy a funnel cake at the fair if you'll eat it." Barry also liked to garden. Although he planted in a somewhat random fashion, we all enjoyed seeing the growth of a large variety of fruits, vegetables, and flowers. Many ideas flooded his mind during his early morning hours of weeding and on his bird-watching walks.

They say opposites attract. Content to care for our family and home, I became the practical half. The one who advocated routine and predictability, I found quieter ways to network with the world. I became a room mother and homework coach. At church, I coordinated a growing ladies' Bible study.

When I found myself pregnant at age thirty-eight, I felt embarrassment mixed with panic. Jana had just turned fourteen and Sharon, eleven. By this time, it seemed parenting presented more challenges than I could successfully manage on some days. And God wanted me to raise another child? Early on, complications landed me on bed rest for over six weeks. I carried the baby all the way to her due date, though, and gave birth to Elisabeth Grace. She was named for Elisabeth Elliot and the promise I clung to in 2 Corinthians 12:9: "My grace is sufficient for you, ..." But God gave me much more than grace. We all adored our little girl. I used to tell her, "I wouldn't trade you for all the peace and quiet in the world."

When we moved to Pennsylvania, a slim housing market in our price range left us with few options, but God provided a house for us within walking distance of the campus. Before Elisabeth turned a year old, we built an addition onto our home—a new garage with a guest room and full bath tucked in the back. *We might need an in-law apartment in the future,* we reasoned. We could never have known that our handicap-accessible room would service *us* more than the occasional guest.

The summer we built the addition to our home, my parents moved to the area. Still in good health, they purchased a home six miles away. My sister lived in Africa by this time. At least, Dad and Mom would live near one of us. I hoped we would not only enjoy frequent visits but be able to help them as they grew older. How could I have ever imagined how the tables would turn in unforeseen ways five short years later?

All too soon, Jana graduated from high school and began college. Sharon continued her college prep courses and involvement at church. She passed her driving test in October of her junior year. That same fall, we enrolled Elisabeth in a preschool enrichment program nearby. I dabbled in poetry writing and even tried a few pieces of prose.

As one day slipped into another, I watched with mixed emotions as our little family changed and grew.

No story stands alone. Before the first paragraph appears on the page, a context already surrounds it. The story behind the story builds a framework, bringing understanding to our circumstances, our responses, our ways of moving forward or grieving loss. Perhaps our past colors the present more than we realize. Perhaps God meant it to be that way.

I'm grateful for my family of origin. I treasure my heritage, my husband, and my children. Yet, there's much more to a family, much more to you and me, than what can be seen from the outside.

CHAPTER TEN

The Good Girl

EVERY STORY, INCLUDING mine, has a quiet, secret side. Behind the observable, a deeper picture evolves from a place hidden to the eyes of even the closest of friends but never to the eyes of God. Here we mull over our motives and fight our fears. We process pain and joy along with nagging questions and silent celebrations.

Some of these unspoken stories eventually spill over into our behavior. Solomon, the wise king of Israel, warned, "Keep *and* guard your heart with all vigilance ... for out of it flow the springs of life."[1] Jesus added, "For out of the overflow of the heart the mouth speaks."[2]

Who we are on the inside comprises a significant part of our stories. The most important part in many ways. This holds true in the present—and also in our backstories.

Authors begin their stories with a bang. They pull us into the plot with action and conflict. We find ourselves drawn to certain characters. But we don't have a full context until the writer adds the backstory, which offers a rich understanding of what led up to the beginning of the book. It provides a frame of reference.

God writes our backstories to prepare us to receive His gifts, to equip us to serve Him, and to train us for the future. He never wastes our backgrounds, seen and unseen, but purposefully redeems them and weaves them into the present. Said another way, we can be "... confident of this, that he who began a good work in you will carry it on to completion until the day of Christ Jesus."[3]

God began His good work in the heart of a little girl from

Buffalo. He has faithfully written my story, inside and out, line by line. And He's still writing.

Backstories

An apostle summarized the story of Jesus this way: "But when the time had fully come, God sent his Son, born of a woman, born under law, to redeem those under law, that we might receive the full rights of sons."[4] Concise and complete, wouldn't you say?

Yet how much richer to read the backstory found in the gospels—the announcement of luminous celestials to earthbound shepherds, telling of a newborn Savior wrapped up warm in a feeding trough. Mysterious kings bowing low before a toddler and offering regal gifts. Scenes of Jesus telling parables to swelling crowds on grassy hillsides ... of Him healing a lame man with mere words and dividing a little boy's lunch to feed thousands ... of His fiery debates with the established religious hierarchy. There's the tender picture of Him asking His closest friend to care for His mother as He hung dying on a Roman cross. And the wonder of that same friend and disciple who ran ahead to find ... an *empty* tomb.

How much fuller yet to understand the Old Testament promise of a Savior from the time of Adam, and then to trace the Messiah's line from Abraham and marvel at the many prophecies fulfilled with exact precision. Backstory makes the story of Jesus sing. We see pictures of His life unfold in living color. And we often get a glimpse into His heart.

Backstory brings stories alive. Connecting the dots between people and their past generates context and adds depth and understanding.

The quiet side of my backstory still leaves me pondering. It links directly to significant personal takeaways as I recovered from my surgeries, as physical therapists signed off on my care, and as I discovered our new normal. This is about more than what happened to us ... to me. It's about how unforeseen traumatic events brought about change, particularly in the hidden places where trust either withers or thrives.

Right and Good

Throughout my life, I've tried hard to be the good girl. I wanted to please my parents and teachers. But more than anything, I longed to please God. The older I grew, the more conscientious I became. I wanted to be right.

As a six-year-old, I listened to the compelling story of Jesus, the Good Shepherd, then joined His flock with a childish, yet sincere, prayer. As a teen, I tossed a stick onto a bonfire at camp, signifying my desire to give my *all* to Christ. I offered my life for missionary service or for *whatever* God might have in mind. These aspirations never left me.

I grew up in the turbulent culture of the 1960s and early seventies. For the most part, society still reflected traditional ethics, concrete dos and don'ts, and rights and wrongs. However, seeds of change found the fertile soil of unrest and growing dissatisfaction with the status quo. As the eighties and nineties pierced the horizon, these seeds began to sprout, forcing the face of society to be forever altered. New ideas challenged long-established principles. Morality fell to new definitions. In the cross fires of these changes, I not only embraced traditional values more tightly, but I unwittingly equated them with the way to become a better Christian.

When three precious little daughters came along, I loved, nurtured, and taught them. As the oldest two girls grew to be teens, the culture—and the church—continued to move left. Caught in the middle of the past and the future, I felt pressure from both extremes and found myself part of the transition generation, struggling to find a reasonable and appropriate balance.

As I continued to emphasize what I considered spiritual ideals, the tensions in our home gradually mounted to the point where conflict became too frequent. This tug-of-war affected our firstborn the most. The distance in our relationship crushed me. I had no idea what to do or where to turn. Were my efforts to be right and good contributing to some of the very walls that separated us?

Rethinking It All

With the help of a Christian counselor, I began a journey to work on my relationships at home. Being the good girl and trying to help my daughters become good girls didn't work the way I thought it should. I relayed the fundamentals of life well, but something was lacking. Forced to rethink my basic tenets, questions swirled in my mind: Were my definitions and traditions in sync with pleasing God or man? Had I been relying on my own rightness rather than on God?

During this time, I came across *The Pursuit of Holiness* by Jerry Bridges.

> Holiness does not consist in mystic speculations, enthusiastic fervours, or uncommanded austerities; it consists in thinking as God thinks, and willing as God wills.[5] Neither does holiness mean, as is so often thought, adhering to a list of "dos and don'ts," mostly don'ts. When Christ came into the world, He said, "I have come to do your will, O God" (Hebrews 10:7). This is the example we are to follow."[6]

As I sifted through the previous chapters of my life, my efforts, and my relationships, it became clear that what I had been striving so hard to achieve was unattainable. No matter how hard I tried, I could not make myself good enough. What I attempted to *do* had already been *done*.

As a little girl, I believed in Jesus Christ, that He died on the cross to save me from my sins, that He rose from the dead. On my forty-second birthday, however, it all took on new meaning. On my knees I prayed, not to be *saved* again, but to confirm that the Christian life isn't about my trying so hard to be good and right. The perfect righteousness of Jesus is credited to me. That alone is the basis for my salvation and the way to do life. In the process of making Jesus, who knew no sin, to be sin for me, God makes me righteous.[7]

To depend on my own endeavors alone proves futile. *God* does the work. In Elisabeth Elliot's words, my responsibility is to "trust and obey."

Growing In Grace

I like the analogy of a child giving a valentine to her parent. Her token of love isn't perfect. Coloring overflows the lines, letters find themselves backward, words are misspelled. But her father doesn't chide her. Instead, he delights in her efforts to express love to him. Each year, as she matures, her father's smile of approval shows how much he treasures every stage of growth.

God's a little like that. My attempts to show love for Him and to please Him often appear out of line, backward. These efforts don't spell C-h-r-i-s-t-i-a-n very well. Many times I misread a situation or my good intentions seem to backfire. But He treasures me as His child and sees past the mistakes and into my heart. He understands and values each stage of growth. Often, He gently takes me by the hand and shows me a more excellent way through His Word. He prompts me to grow in grace and points me back to the basics: to love God and love my neighbor.

After traveling fifty-some years on the pathway of life, I'll probably always lean to the conventional side. It's who I am. I value being comfortable with who He made me to be and allowing others the freedom to be who they are. Each person has a unique story worthy of my respect.

As society continues to shift, this is my aspiration: to honor my heritage and, at the same time, to dance with the inevitable changes ahead. I want the Master Writer to guide the pencil and write my life story as I seek "to do *your* will, O my God."

This part of my backstory represents a significant paradigm shift from trying so hard to please God to a deeper understanding of His work in my life. But God, who had lovingly begun His work in me, desired to bring me farther ... to draw me closer ... to increase my trust in Him. Less than three years from the time God brought Jerry Bridges' book to my attention, the car crash and its repercussions acted as a catalyst to open my eyes wider to the implications of my compliant "good-girl approach" to life.

Your Story

God has shaped *your* backstory to prepare your present as it affects your future. He will not allow your background or your past to be wasted, whether its influence is seen or unseen. Create a timeline of your life. Jot down your heritage and significant events, including important relationships, experiences, relocations, and major decisions. In another color, add in your spiritual, inner journey. Note your relationship with God, significant steps of growth, and paradigm shifts. Thank God for His good work in your life. Meditate on what you've learned in chapters nine and ten about your visible and less-visible backstory. Write a prayer or a story of trust. Refer to Philippians 1:6 and Psalm 40:6-8.

PART THREE

ESTABLISHING OUR NEW NORMAL
MAY 8, 2003 – APRIL 5, 2004, AND BEYOND

CHAPTER ELEVEN

Two Hats

I GINGERLY—AND TEARFULLY—STEPPED over the threshold into our dining room. With that one single step, I left the hospital scene behind and entered a new chapter of our story. In my halo, I pushed my walker from room to room, savoring the familiar, grateful—after thirty-five days—to be home with my children.

When my hospital bed arrived, we decided to have it set up in the guest room addition we had built. My parents planned to stay with us, but the girls, then twenty, seventeen, and five, insisted they could care for me just fine. They found a bell for me to ring in case I needed anything during the night. Dad and Mom filled prescriptions for muscle relaxants and narcotic-strength painkillers, and the girls made a chart for me to keep my medications straight.

I needed help caring for the bedsore on the back of my head and cleaning my four pin sites, the places where the halo screwed into my skull. The risk of infection remained a daily danger. Blood thinners necessitated frequent trips to the lab. In addition, the calendar already reflected outpatient physical therapy three times a week. I felt grateful—and guilty—for depending on my parents, Jana, and friends to take me to one appointment after another.

Over the next weeks and months, people's eagerness to help us meant lovingly prepared meals delivered with care and concern. Neighbors and colleagues cut our grass. Another preschool mom chauffeured Elisabeth to school. Two nurse-friends from church volunteered to help me shower on a rotating basis; one arrived after working all night. My hairdresser came to the house, working around my halo with humor and ease. My more practical friends brought paper goods and grocery staples. Some offered to babysit.

And sometimes I found flowers—bouquets quietly attached to the handle of our back door. God must have whispered the idea into the hearts of those who brought them as they seemed to appear when fatigue and raw nerves got the best of me.

The outpouring of love and support from church, the college where Barry worked, and our community overwhelmed me, but repeatedly having to receive felt humbling and uncomfortable. I endeavored to give back what I could: a smile, a positive word, a blessing to those who gave with unforgettable kindness and generosity.

Forging Ahead

Soon, our mailbox overflowed with medical bills for all four of us. Barry had always handled our finances, yet I had no choice but to take on this daunting task, one bill at a time. Because our car insurance's medical benefit ran out even before our helicopters landed, I needed to make numerous calls to clarify our health insurance information. On each bill, I jotted down the gist of my conversation and placed it in one of the piles on the dining room table. I kept track of co-pays, paid our usual bills, balanced our checkbook, and marveled at God's provision.

I made follow-up appointments for Sharon and Elisabeth with their primary care physicians and took them to an understanding counselor who helped them process the car crash and all that happened. My family doctor not only took over my care and regulated my meds but reassured me, explaining the whys and wherefores. I had someone to confer with when my left side felt numb, while the sharp, stabbing pain of pins and needles kept me on edge, and when lower back pain and muscle spasms plagued me. My physical therapist put me through the paces necessary to gradually regain my strength.

The day finally came when I could walk *without* my walker.

A Mother's Heart

Not long after returning home, Sharon attended the junior/senior banquet sponsored by her school. We had purchased her outfit and had it altered before our trip—a soft, flowing green dress that accentuated her slender figure and delicate features. Sharon had always loved dressing up, and this was no exception. She looked lovely. But Barry, at the nursing home and still unaware of the outside world—let alone his daughter's activities—couldn't be there.

My heart ached for our daughter whose dad would've said, "Give me a twirl, hon ... very nice." After the banquet, Sharon laid down beside me in bed and took a picture of the two of us, her in her pretty dress and me in my halo. I loved hearing all about her evening.

Sharon often cleaned my pin sites. She ensured I had everything I needed at bedtime and made a point to play quiet, classical music before she left my room. "Good night, Momma," she'd say. "I love you. Ring the bell if you need anything."

That's when the tears I'd kept in check all day finally slid down my cheeks and wet my pillow. I prayed that God would sustain Sharon with His grace. I asked Him to help Jana as she made up her classwork and maintained her job. I pleaded with God to give me the ability to be a good mother to little Elisabeth. And I wondered how long I would go to bed in one location and my husband in another? What did the future hold? Once more, I prayed for Barry's healing.

Fears and Uncertainties

In time, we managed to establish somewhat of a routine. But a few challenging memories still haunt me. Riding in a car brought my pulse rate up while my eyes darted every which way. We had a twenty-five-minute drive one way to see Barry at Mountain View Care Center. When he transferred to John Heinz Institute for a more specialized brain injury rehab program, the time lengthened to forty-five minutes.

One day on our way home, rain fell in sheets, beating on the windshield and greatly reducing our visibility. With my heart pounding, I asked the driver if it would be best to pull over. She thought it would be safer to keep going. Feeling helpless and vulnerable, I clung to the seat and prayed. I arrived home safely but deeply shaken. How could God allow this to happen after all we'd been through? The only answer I received hung on the handle of the back door. I watered those flowers with my tears as I brought them into the house. God knew all about it.

About a month after I came home, the screws on my halo loosened. I panicked. No one told me this often happens or what to do if it did. With my surgeons five hours away, Jana took me to the ER of a nearby hospital, but they had no experience with halos. Finally, they contacted a neurosurgeon who gave them over-the-phone instructions—to no avail. We had to come back to the ER the next day when he would be there to make the adjustments. It felt like fire when he tightened the screws, but it worked—for about eighteen days. The second time I felt the screws loosening, my parents took me back to the doctor in Johnstown where I traded my halo—a little early—for a rigid neck brace with its own set of limitations, to be worn for eight more weeks.

Counting Our Blessings

From the time I arrived home, I kept a journal of praise and thankfulness. Already, we had so much for which to thank God. I knew if I didn't record His blessings, many of them would be forgotten. Sometimes I wrote more, but on most days I jotted down a line or two. This became the most enlightening resource for writing this part of our story.

Our day-by-day account reveals a list of the wonderful friends who provided meals and rides, visited Barry, sent us the proceeds of their garage sales, and helped in a hundred different ways. I kept a log of celebrations and disappointments, large and small. I also jotted down setbacks, test results, relational conflicts, and reconciliations. When faith gave way to fear, this objective journal of God's faithfulness calmed me down and helped me focus on the positives rather than all the unknowns. Each entry represents a picture of God's abundant provision for a family who needed to trust Him more than ever.

The Other Hat

Something happened every time I stepped across the threshold of Mountain View Care Center during the five weeks Barry was there. Outside, I was the patient, wearing a halo, recovering from a broken neck. Once inside, however, I traded hats. As Barry's wife and medical power of attorney, I felt the weighty oversight of his care.

Pallid and too thin, the man who had a one-in-a-million

chance of recovery woke up, gradually at first as from a deep sleep. When conscious, he became agitated and fiddled with his trach. We noticed he didn't open his eyes much, but his verbal responses increased little by little as he became more attentive to his environment. Even in his confusion, he started to recognize us and seemed to look forward to our visits. Within a week of his arrival at the nursing facility, two therapists had him up and walking, one on each side. He had trouble swallowing, so required a feeding tube and thickened water and juice.

I became protective of my college vice president husband who had seven academic degrees after his name but now rambled like a child. This was *not* the time for curious company. I requested no visitors but asked a few people closest to us to spend some time with him. They graciously picked me up en route. Barry enjoyed these interactions and recognized everyone who came.

His intelligence and drive worked to his advantage. Soon, he began to participate in multiple therapies designed to help brain-injured patients. Photos of family members, our home, and the college scene, all placed in a scrapbook, helped re-acclimate him to his former environment.

With mixed emotions, I watched my husband, formerly so capable and proficient, work with shapes and puzzles, simple mind exercises, and word games. Basic preschool-level activities soon gave way to elementary-level challenges.

His core muscles and limbs became stronger. We cheered him on. But he had a hard time communicating and found himself stuck, repeating the same words and phrases. He struggled with balance when he walked and navigated steps. And his eyesight was an ongoing issue.

The staff at Mountain View enjoyed the challenge of helping Barry progress and even hung a bird feeder outside his window because he had loved bird-watching. They provided ample opportunities for him to exercise both mind and body. When they gave him therapeutic feedings to test his swallowing, he kept saying over and over, "This is gloorrrrious!" His weight had dropped into the low 140s on his 6'2" frame. I waited impatiently for the day when his improved ability to swallow finally allowed him to eat three square meals a day.

Because he was a fall risk and policy prohibited the use of restraints, Barry could not be left alone. The staff often wheeled him out to the nurses' station so they could keep an eye on him—especially in the very early mornings. Toward the end of his stay, he joked with the nurses and requested ice cream before breakfast, which they often gave him. Again and again, he asked when he could call me. They finally handed him the phone at 6:30 a.m.

"Hi, Sarah," he'd say when he called. "When are you coming?"

"Good morning, hon. How about 10:00?"

"Could you expedite that?"

Expedite? Barry's vocabulary from the past cropped up in funny, unexpected ways. The girls and I often smiled over the things he said. We also took note of even the smallest steps of improvement.

One day, less than two months after the crash, he wrote me a love note—one of my most priceless treasures, now framed in my office. "Dear Sarahahah. I love youe very much! Love muchly."

I love you, too, hon. You're doing great. Keep marching forward.

CHAPTER TWELVE

The Power of Story

THE DAYS CYCLED into weeks. I went to physical therapy, paid the bills, wrote thank-you notes, made phone calls, showed up for appointments, cleaned my pin sites, took my medications, and worked out transportation to see Barry. Most evenings, after tucking Elisabeth into bed, I found solace in picking up a book. I read a few delightful volumes of *The Mitford Series* by Jan Karon, Elisabeth Elliot's reassuring collection titled *Secure in the Everlasting Arms,* and, of course, Gracia Burnham's powerful story of courage, *In the Presence of My Enemies,* which continues to inspire me.

The power of story touches us all.

How many times have I pulled a book off the shelf, searching for answers to my dilemmas, seeking support from someone else's experiences? I identify with those having similar sufferings and look for how they persevered. These authors often quote other stories in their writings. We all benefit from the experiences of others.

God uses stories to comfort us and give us hope. I've found the Bible full of compelling narratives that attest to God's care for His children. Christians down through the ages have shared their personal accounts of God's faithfulness. These have strengthened my trust in the One who is writing my life story with a loving providence that offers a higher perspective, no matter what happens.

The evenings spent reading and reflecting strengthened me during the busy, hectic days and the long sleepless nights. As my physical body healed, God also brought His healing touch to my heart.

That We Might Have Hope

Near the end of his letter to the Roman Christians, the apostle Paul unexpectedly slipped in an intriguing idea about story. "For everything that was written in the past was written to teach us, so that through endurance and the encouragement of the Scriptures we might have hope."[1]

One of Paul's stories caught my attention. Set in the province of Asia, he shared:

We were under great pressure, far beyond our ability to endure, so that we despaired even of life. Indeed, in our hearts we felt the sentence of death. *But this happened that we might not rely on ourselves but on God, who raises the dead.* He has delivered us from such a deadly peril, and he will deliver us. On him we have set our hope ... as you help us by your prayers. Then many will give thanks on our behalf for the gracious favor granted us in answer to the prayers of many.[2]

Perhaps our family's circumstances would increase our dependence on God and His deliverance. I prayed it would be so.

Reading story after story in the Scriptures brought my focus upward, from the healing of an unnamed woman in Luke 13 to the heroes of faith in Hebrews 11. And in His providence, God brought the victories of certain others across my path to draw me to Himself.

Grab Bars of Faith

Elisabeth Elliot's straightforward encouragement to "trust and obey" simplified the seeming complexity of my questions during these weeks. The account of her husband's martyrdom and of her subsequent missionary work gave her writings credibility.[3] I read through her books with a highlighter.

"Everything is an affair of the spirit," Mrs. Elliot writes. "If eating and drinking can be done 'to the glory of God' (1 Corinthians 10:31 KJV) so can everything else."[4] I wrote in the margin: *like wearing a halo!*

From the very beginning, my halo represented an unrelenting

part of my healing regime. Unable to move my head, I learned to use my eyes more or bend from the waist to either look down or turn to face someone beside me. Forced to lie only on my back in bed without changing positions, I often couldn't sleep. I had to sit straight without using the back of a chair. The thought of feeling so restricted by the halo—and the brace around my middle—for three whole months left me feeling uneasy and apprehensive.

I found great comfort after realizing I had to wear it only *today*. One day at a time. In my reading I underlined these words: "When we try to meet difficulties prematurely we have neither the light nor the strength for them yet."[5] Moses voiced a similar thought: "As thy days, so shall thy strength be."[6]

Mrs. Elliot's writings also advocated doing "the next thing."[7] I often worried about the many unknowns regarding Barry's care, my own health, and specific concerns related to the girls. Yet doing the next thing often meant the ordinary tasks of making lunch, getting ready for an appointment, or reading a story to Elisabeth. Focusing on one step at a time made life simpler. It helped me trust God for the present duty at hand—and for the future as it came.

Jim O'Donell, whose wife developed an aggressive form of cancer, wrote a letter to Mrs. Elliot, which she quotes in her book. His words made a lasting impression on me:

We must learn how to be faithful people in this new assignment, … There is a whole new vocabulary we are coming to know, one we never would have wanted to know anything about. … God can heal. But we also trust that even serious illness can serve God's good and holy purposes to arouse love and care in others, to turn our trust from ourselves to Him, and maybe spur some to reflect on what truly is important in life.[8]

In the busyness of my days, I found myself mulling over these truths. Simple principles, really. But they gave me something to steady my mind when I felt my balance slipping. They helped me to better accept our situation, and they strengthened my sometimes tentative trust in God, who scatters hope into our stories.

Tenacity in the Chapel

Down the hall from Barry's room at Mountain View, a large chapel beckoned residents to socialize and attend special programs and religious services. Only a few chairs lined the back wall as wheelchairs made up the seating. This became Barry's place.

When musicians performed, he sang along and clapped to the music. He played bingo and even attended mass. He seemed happy at Mountain View—oblivious to my injuries, the stacks of bills, or concerns for his future.

Barry used his feet to wheel himself into the empty chapel. After several weeks, we'd often find him walking back and forth, back and forth, trying to regain his strength and balance. Remarkably, he never fell. Elisabeth liked to wheel herself around in his chair. In this sacred place, he first comprehended what happened to us in the accident and squeezed my hand with tears running down his face. I'll always treasure that sweet time with just the two of us. "Can you write to all these people [who helped us] and tell them thank you?" he asked.

A couple days later, Barry apologized for "being this way." Increasingly aware of his deficits, he added with growing awareness, "I'll have to slow down."

A month after his arrival, I asked if our family could use the chapel for our annual end-of-the-school-year lunch. The five of us held hands around the table. Barry prayed as tears of thanksgiving dampened our cheeks. After we ate, Barry passed out gifts for all of us—pens with an artificial flower attached by floral tape—he had made in therapy. He remembered our tradition and seemed pleased to be able to contribute. Consistent with our custom, I acknowledged specific character qualities—Jana, loyalty (Isaiah 40:30, 31); Sharon, stability (Isaiah 26:3); Elisabeth, courage (Joshua 1:9). And for Barry, Isaiah 40:29: "He gives strength to the weary and increases the power of the weak."

About that same time, my dad went alone to visit Barry. No two men could be more opposite than Barry and Dad. Barry's ambitious personality collided with Dad's sensitive, artistic bent. Sometimes I sensed tension between the two of them. This particular day, my dad asked for Barry's forgiveness. He felt he could have been a better father-in-law. They shed tears and prayed together—a new beginning for their relationship.

On June 12, thirty-five days after arriving in a semi-comatose state, Barry was ready to leave Mountain View for the next level of care. A bittersweet day for us all. Along with our family, the staff there had witnessed nothing short of a miracle.

Doing the Next Thing

Barry transferred to John Heinz Institute of Rehabilitation and stayed for ten days. John Heinz didn't offer the same homey, personal atmosphere as Mountain View, but they provided a more rigorous level of therapy and began the process of pinpointing the problem with Barry's eyes. The ophthalmologist confirmed that he had double vision caused by damage to his optic nerve. They provided him with an eye patch to cover first one eye, then the other, back and forth. We hoped, in time, the two images would come together as normal.

Barry participated in physical, occupational, and speech therapy every day, all day. The social workers offered patient families the opportunity to watch an informative documentary on traumatic brain injury. It revealed some of the many challenges we would face in the days ahead. But even then, I didn't know what I didn't know.

Soon, Barry would come home. I felt grateful and apprehensive at the same time. Yet I remembered the stories, the heroes of faith, the writings of Paul, Gracia Burnham, and Elisabeth Elliot. I would need their reminders to reach upward toward hope. I would seek their wisdom as I sought to trust God with this next chapter of our lives.

Your Story

God uses stories to offer comfort and hope. Meditate on what you've learned in chapters eleven and twelve about how the experiences of others offer the tools you need to move forward. What biblical characters have modeled perseverance and given you strength in your circumstances? Name a few non-biblical stories or books that have bolstered your faith and heightened your trust in God. What specific principles have made a difference in your perspective and offered you hope? Write a prayer or a story of trust. Refer to Romans 15:4; 1 Corinthians 10:11; and 2 Timothy 3:16, 17.

CHAPTER THIRTEEN

The Next Chapter

EVEN BEFORE WE had an exact date, the countdown to Barry's homecoming sent me scurrying to get ready. I wanted everything to be caught up and in order. More than that, I wanted him to feel welcome and at home.

Once again, Barry's sister and niece made their way from Michigan to Pennsylvania, this time to visit Barry at John Heinz. They walked with him around the courtyard and observed him in the therapy room. At home, they helped us prepare for Barry's arrival. They scrubbed our guest room from top to bottom and set up the guest room bed near my hospital bed. Their visit could not have come at a better time.

A few days before Barry came home, Sharon joined the church youth group as they traveled to North Carolina for a missions trip. She and I had debated if she should go as planned, due to her dad's impending discharge from John Heinz, but we decided it might be good for her to get away. Pastor Frank and his wife, Kim, chaperoned the trip, and I knew Sharon would be in good hands. Perhaps a change in focus would offer some healing.

On June 21, eleven weeks after we left for vacation, Barry took his turn crossing the threshold into our dining room. Wearing his eye patch, he wandered around, relishing the feeling of home. I watched him with a weepy smile, overcome by the miracle of it all. We prepared his favorite foods: shrimp cocktail, hamburgers, and homemade fries topped off with strawberries from his garden—a bumper crop that year.

From Halo to Neck Brace

Soon after, my parents drove me back to Johnstown to get my

halo removed. The physician's assistant asked if I wanted to take it home with me. "No, thank you!" I laughed, so thrilled to shed this chapter of my treatment. I came home with a rigid neck brace that would allow me to finally sleep on my side. I could take it off in the summer heat as long as I did *not* move my head in *any* direction—not one iota. But the brace lifted my head higher than the halo and would need to be worn twice as long as I anticipated. Would this *ever* be over? I wrote in my journal, *Grieving the loss of expectations continues to be a challenge.* On the positive side, my disappointment was tempered by the finish of rehab therapy. Another stepping stone on a bumpy journey.

Growing Stronger

It didn't take long to notice that Barry became easily fatigued, a discouragement for him for many months to come. He needed frequent naps and rest periods, but his strength continued to increase. About seven weeks after his return home, he could mow part of our small lawn—*if* the neighbor started the mower.

Barry's rehabilitation continued at John Heinz, forty-five minutes away. Three mornings a week, he labored to regain his mental and physical capacities—always with one eye, due to the alternating patch. Co-workers, church members, and community friends willingly picked him up, waited all morning, then brought him home at lunch time. He did not miss one out-patient appointment all the way through those four months until his therapies ended.

God's Provision

Through the course of those first weeks and months at home, Barry became more involved in household activities and duties, including our finances. He fretted about getting another car, the possibility of using up our savings, and not having enough for our day-to-day expenses. No matter how much I shared with him about God supplying our needs over the past weeks, he couldn't let it go. My frustration mounted. I had paid the bills, written the checks, made the calls. I had seen the hand of God supply.

But ... what if his fears came to fruition?

A knowing smile must have spread across the face of God the morning it all came to a head, because the next day we received a check in the mail for $3000. Years before, we had loaned a couple money and agreed they would pay us back when they could. When they moved away, the loan slipped our minds—until that moment. The check, together with the insurance money for our totaled Toyota, would enable us to buy another car—a Subaru Legacy.

After our brush with death, I felt an urgency to pursue the truly important, to do what really matters. I pondered the warning of Jesus when He said, "Watch out! Be on your guard ... a man's life does not consist in the abundance of his possessions."[1] And Paul's words, "Set your minds on things above, not on earthly things."[2]

Barry and I both knew we needed to simplify. We listed our four-acre property in the country. Barry gave boxes of theology books to a young local pastor and a Bible school in India. He asked a contractor to take some extra wood and roof tiles from the garage.

Later that fall, we did pull from our savings to keep up with the co-pays and bills. Remembering the pictures of God's provision helped us trust that He would continue to supply our needs when we needed a new kitchen faucet, when the furnace for our addition needed to be replaced, and when our second car gave out.

Back to Church

The first time we went to church after the crash, Sharon, our designated driver, took a quick photo of Barry and me by our front gate. Elisabeth was grinning, her arm around my waist. How wonderful to walk into church and see many of the friends who had helped us ... friends who organized prayer meetings on our behalf, sent cards, supplied suppers, gave rides, loaned us an air conditioner, and on and on. The music in the service put a lump in my throat as did the many gentle hugs we received.

In the midst of our joy, we discovered something about Barry's hearing. Everything sounded disturbingly loud to him. Too many voices in one place seemed chaotic and confusing. The music in our church demonstrated restraint and balance, and we sat near the back, but Barry wore earplugs on Sunday mornings for a long time.

Our church held a special praise service to thank God for His answers to prayer both for us and for Dennis Wilhite, a college colleague who had recovered from a brain tumor removal about the same time as our accident. Neighbors, friends, and family joined together to praise God for His gracious miracles and for doing immeasurably more than all we could ask or imagine.[3] Singing "Great is Thy Faithfulness" still reminds me of that wonderful evening.

Picking Up My Pen Again

During my recovery and after we welcomed Barry home, Mom and I attended a local Christian writers' conference.[4] I had written a little poetry during Elisabeth's preschool years and had commuted to the conference the two previous summers. When I entered the chapel in my neck brace, the worship music surrounded me like an oasis in the desert. I nearly wept in the aisle. Not only could I take a break from all the responsibility I carried each day, I felt the support of these dear writer friends who had heard about our situation and prayed for us. Little did I know I would someday bring *this story* to the writers' conference for acceptance and publication.

Seeing Beyond the Here and Now

The ophthalmologist confirmed Barry's observation that his vision seemed to be normal when he looked straight ahead, but when he looked down through his bifocals, he saw double. Prisms in his lenses could not merge the two images because one image was at an angle. He tried the patch over one eye, tape over one bifocal, and a change in prescription, but nothing proved satisfactory. Besides this issue, his pupils did not contract and expand as they should. The local doctors sent us to Wills Eye Hospital in Philadelphia for a specialist's opinion. The doctor there confirmed our fears. No surgery or procedure could correct the problem.

This translated into a staggering loss, especially for a man who loved learning, books, and all things academic. We prayed and prayed for another miracle. However, God did not heal Barry's ever-present diplopia, which not only caused eye fatigue and poor vision but also affected reading, eating, walking, keeping his balance, playing sports, shoveling snow, gardening, and doing computer work. Basically, everything.

Now, the future seemed more muddled than ever. We found ourselves discouraged and disheartened. I clung to these words from the pen of Paul: "Therefore we do not lose heart. Though outwardly we are wasting away, yet inwardly we are being renewed day by day. For our light and momentary troubles are achieving for us an eternal glory that far outweighs them all. *So we fix our eyes not on what is seen, but on what is unseen. For what is seen is temporary, but what is unseen is eternal.*"[5]

Barry found multiple ways to compensate. While working in his garden or taking a walk, he often listened to the Bible and a variety of books on CD. He held newspapers and books straight ahead when reading. He enlarged the print on his computer and used a flat-screen positioned up high. He wore a good pair of sunglasses whenever leaving the house. Because he didn't complain, people he met never knew. This was Barry's preference, but every waking hour he would literally stare his losses in the face.

Perhaps the miracle does not always come in the healing but in God giving us a day-by-day capacity to accept our limitations ... to make the best of our challenges and trust that somehow God has a plan in it all.

On the Road Again

When my neck vertebrae had completely healed—about four and a half months after the crash—my doctor granted clearance to gradually wean myself off the neck brace. Talk about a stiff neck ... After looking only straight ahead for so long, my muscles felt stuck. Every day and little by little, I could move my head a bit more, up and down, side to side. It took several weeks to find a normal range of motion.

We returned my hospital bed, and Barry and I moved ourselves back into our bedroom upstairs. We had to be careful navigating the steps, but I treasured the warmth of lying beside the man I had almost lost.

Being discharged from treatment also meant I could drive again, but the thought of it found me wringing my hands. "I'll help you, Mom," Sharon encouraged me. "We'll practice in the church parking lot. I know you can do it." This from the girl who had no choice but to get back in the driver's seat after her nightmare in the fog five months before. I marveled at the grace of God in her life.

Reluctantly, I followed her to the car. My responsibilities beckoned. I had to get behind the wheel again. I couldn't let my apprehension paralyze me. Sharon, in her gentle way, coached me around the parking lot, around the block, and around town. Her generous words of kindness made it safe for me to acknowledge my fears while nudging me toward courage and confidence.

As summer faded into fall and we headed toward the holidays, I came to realize that God was using our situation to influence the lives of those around us in a greater way than we would ever know.

CHAPTER FOURTEEN

A Different Voice

BY THE TIME Barry came home, I thought we'd been through the worst.

Looking back over the course of the ten weeks following the day of the crash, we'd come miles in our recovery. We fought our way back with multiple surgeries, weeks of rehab, and all that modern medicine had to offer. Finally, as a family, we ate together at our own dinner table—the result of God's faithfulness, paired with hard work and determination.

In this new chapter, we discovered that sometimes the greatest challenges occur when and where we least expect them. They crop up as shadowy images, competing with our brightest blessings. We can find ourselves reeling from their impact and disappointed with our inability to cope.

The car crash changed us all. For Barry, his injuries altered the way he thought and felt, the way he related to people, and the way he viewed himself.

There's a vast difference between the repercussions of a traumatic brain stem injury and the effects of broken bones, collapsed lungs, neuropathy, or even altered vision. The brain controls countless functions, including personality, emotions, relational skills, and the ability to handle stress. Brain injury alters these same areas of behavior.

We expected Barry to have issues related to his injuries. We expected him to need rehabilitation and assistance in his recovery. We expected he would require our help at home. But no book or documentary could prepare us for the first weeks and months of his homecoming. Maybe we should have anticipated the difficulties or asked additional questions. We could have learned more about our family's role in the process. Bottom line: Barry's behaviors revealed a different voice.

Each of my writer friends writes with a certain "voice" or style that reflects their unique identity. In a similar way, each of us lives out our life stories with a God-given voice. He created our personalities, our talents, and our bent. We are "fearfully and wonderfully made."[1] We all fluctuate and grow to a certain extent, but normally the backbone of our personhood doesn't change much. A shy introvert seldom turns into a sanguine salesman. A person's character can change, but the basics stay somewhat predictable.

And we get used to relating to each other this way.

Before the crash, we saw Barry as the leader, the driver, the decisive and knowledgeable head of our family. When the fog hit, the first words out of my mouth were: "Barry, it's foggy." I expected him to lean forward from the backseat and help Sharon through the crisis—which he would have done had he not been absorbed in a book.

Before the crash, Barry related to me in a certain way, as well as to each of the girls and vice versa. Not flawlessly of course, yet we each felt comfortable in our respective, predictable patterns. But after the crash, Barry's voice changed. Family roles became mixed up. Who did the caregiving now? Who depended on whom? And how did these changes and challenges affect our relationships with each other?

The Woman Who Lost It All

A family unit resembles the human body. "If one part suffers, every part suffers with it; if one part is honored, every part rejoices with it."[2] Whatever happens to one affects all the others. When trauma strikes a family, the cumulative effects can be staggering.

Our losses cannot compare to the devastation Job faced, yet I find myself intrigued by his story. His résumé listed titles including husband, father of ten, successful businessman, and "the greatest man among all the people of the East." Besides maintaining a blameless and upright character, "he feared God and shunned evil." He regularly prayed for his children.[3]

Then trouble hit. He lost 1000 oxen, 500 donkeys, 3000 camels to raiding parties, and 7000 sheep to fire. Plus, he lost the servants who cared for them all. A "mighty wind" caused his oldest son's house to collapse, killing all ten of his children who had gathered there.

Everything gone. All in one day.

And if all that didn't cause enough grief, Job developed painful, itchy sores from head to toe. His friends hardly recognized him as he sat in the ashes, grief-stricken and alone.

I tried to look at his story through the eyes of Job's wife. What did it feel like to lose *all* their financial security at once? Then *all* ten of their dear children? Perhaps she pictured each one's precious face, one by one, as her desperate wailing echoed through the village. Overcome and alone, she saw her soul mate in his deplorable condition, and she cried out, "Are you still holding on to your integrity? Curse God and die!"[4]

Not the right thing to say, according to Job, who named her among the "foolish" who accepted good from God and not trouble.[5]

Probably *not* the right thing to say, but it makes me wonder ... what would *I* have said if all this happened to me? In that moment, would I have been able to muster up a few words of blessing? Of loyalty, at least? Or would grief swallow me to the point of anger and despair?

When someone in the family suffers, we all suffer. Sometimes we say things we shouldn't say. Sometimes we blurt out emotions we later regret. We each pass through the varying stages of grief—denial, anger, bargaining, depression, acceptance—in different ways and at different times.

Our family was no exception.

Under the Same Roof

Living under the same roof heightened our awareness of just how much life had changed for all of us. I observed each of our daughters grieve her particular losses in a different way. With good intentions, I tried to listen and help them work through their adjustments but often felt overwhelmed with how to do it well.

Sharon had been away on the missions trip the first week after Barry's discharge from John Heinz. A few days after she returned, I asked how she felt about her dad being home, how she thought it was going. She laid her head in my lap and sobbed.

She knew it would be different, but the reality was more difficult than she imagined. Her dad acted so much older, like her grandpa. She watched him struggle with balance, fret over our finances, and express frustration over taking his medication. We chatted about the importance of taking time to grieve. We had no way of knowing whether she and her dad would ever again connect with daddy-daughter dates or summertime hikes. Our talk benefited both of us, really. Every once in a while, I checked in with her and encouraged our quiet, hold-it-all-in daughter to voice her feelings and opinions.

Jana, on the other hand, had no problem articulating her concerns. And in the process, our relationship slid backward, adding yet another layer of strain to the family dynamic. She hated her time at home, seeing her dad worry excessively about his job, his deficits, and even her. She resisted his advice about everything from career goals to windshield wipers. Later in the fall, she admitted, "I hate the way it is. I used to be able to talk to Dad about these things."

When Jana left for work, I'd often tell her, "We're fine, hon." While I meant we'd be okay while she went out, she often took offense. "Quit saying everything is fine. It's not. This family is falling apart!" Once or twice, she called me a few minutes after leaving the house. "I'm not trying to be upset with you. I get so frustrated. I know you can't do anything about it. I just want you to listen."

Elisabeth voiced her own grief that summer. Barry struggled to re-establish his place as the father figure in her life. He played with her, and together they read the children's versions of *Pilgrim's Progress* and *Hind's Feet on High Places*. One day I found her upset in her bed. There had been some sort of tiff between them. "Why can't Daddy be like he used to be?" she asked through her sobs. "Why did the accident change everything? Why does it have to be so hard?" She caught her breath, tears streaming down her cheeks. "When will Dad be like my daddy used to be?"

I pulled our perceptive little girl into my arms and rocked her as we cried together. I didn't have any answers, but I assured her that our *heavenly* Father is perfect. He cares for us and loves us, even when it's hard. He *never* changes. God invites us to become part of His family and spend forever in heaven with Him where there are no tears and no hurt—and where Daddy would be all better again.

I found the emotions of the girls overwhelming and didn't always know how to encourage them. Challenging as it was, I knew they needed to share how they felt. I cared deeply about their part of the story. We all needed to talk it out in order to begin the healing process.

But as the days slipped into weeks, I felt increasingly isolated and alone. I tossed and turned at night. What did trusting God look like now?

Sorting Out the Pieces

The many conversations with the girls—along with my own struggles—filled the pages of my journal throughout the remainder of 2003. I recorded insights, quotes, and Scriptures that resonated with me, ideas I didn't want to forget, principles that perhaps God wanted me to carry into the future.

Jana's comments reminded me of the tension between striving for normalcy and acknowledging the losses. I wanted to avoid one extreme of saying, "We're fine, fine, fine" and the opposite extreme of wallowing in our circumstances. I prayed God would help us find the balance.

Around the time I journaled about feeling sad, overwhelmed, fearful, and burned out, a dear friend sent a note:

Hi, Sarah, I've tried to catch your eye [in church] recently. You've had a faraway look. I'm sure I don't know all that's going on, but I know enough to realize you're carrying a load. Sarah, please choose thankfulness over anger or pity. God _is_ faithful!

I felt rebuked by her words, but I needed them. How easy to slip away from the basics of gratefulness and trust.

I often wrote out prayers asking God, *What does faithfulness look like now? How can I please you?* Again, Elisabeth Elliot's book gave me perspective. "The pathway to holiness is located right where you are. In those circumstances, those relationships, in that tiredness, in that challenge. The grace of God to make you holy is right there."[6]

Right here ... under the same roof.

I had seen God bring our family together from a trauma that could have ended much differently … a trauma that changed each one of us. The neuropsychologist said Barry would continue to improve for at least two years. Maybe faithfulness meant taking my husband's hand and walking closely beside him and the girls as they each tried to discover the new normal in their stories—in *our* story.

Hadn't God promised I could trust His sufficient grace … for them … and for me? Grace sufficient enough for me to choose thankfulness and trust in the One who writes our stories with purpose and hope.

Your Story

Each person lives out his or her life story with a God-given voice. Meditate on what you've learned in chapters thirteen and fourteen about how a change in voice affects relationships, especially within a family. What can you take away from the story of Job and his wife? How does having someone to listen ease the process of grief? How do thankfulness and trust help you in the midst of your losses? What does faithfulness to God look like for you during this chapter of your life? Write a prayer or a story of trust. Refer to Job 1:1-2:13 and 42:1-17; Psalm 139:14; 1 Corinthians 12:26.

CHAPTER FIFTEEN

In Sickness and in Health

As determined as I was to walk with Barry and cheer him on, I didn't always do it well.

Gradually, the reality of our limitations became clear—*not* what I considered an ideal picture. It's not that I didn't feel grateful for all God had done for us. I thanked Him every day. But I found our day-in and day-out new normal overwhelming. Besides the ramifications of my own injuries, I didn't know how to relate to my husband, so unlike his former self. Why did my role seem like half wife and half mother? Why did I find myself repeatedly running to the other side of the boat to balance him out? Why couldn't I better handle the changes?

At the doctor's request, I kept an account of Barry's progress— his victories and his deficits. I never shared his challenges with anyone except the medical staff and sometimes my mom who listened patiently without holding a single grudge.

Suffice it to say, Barry's injuries weakened the usual filters we develop as we learn acceptable behaviors. These filters restrain and inhibit impulses in the name of good judgment or defer to a higher priority. Barry needed cues to help him in multiple areas. He tended toward the extremes of too much or too little. He often switched his opinion within a matter of hours. His personality change affected the way he processed life.

But I had changed too. In the vacuum, I gained more confidence. I made the decision *not* to pull the plug. I handled the bills, dealt with insurance companies, managed the house, and connected with the girls. I kept my chin up in the darkest of times, all the while trying to recover from my own issues. Perhaps the voice I developed symbolized a healthy change, but it represented one more dynamic we all had to get used to.

I missed Barry's leadership, his direction, and his stability. I did my best to help him, but we did not always see eye to eye. My frustrations often turned to resentment. I put up walls to protect myself. And for the first time since the crash, I found myself angry.

A Safe Place to Heal

I never blamed the people whose cars crashed into ours. They couldn't see through the fog any better than we could. Even the physician who recommended that we discontinue the respirator thought he acted in our best interest. To this point, I had gone from one crisis to another, trying to do the next thing and the next and the next. But now, like dense fog, the reality of it all engulfed me.

A wise counselor once shared that anger is a secondary emotion. Anger stems from pain, frustration, or fear. Now I understood this more than ever. I still dealt with daily physical pain. I also experienced hurt due to some of Barry's reactions, which came from emotions I had never seen in him before. I felt frustrated and even trapped with the seeming lack of progress. Alongside the ever-present dread of getting into a car, I wondered how long it would take to get beyond this point in our relationship.

Trauma can bring out our best ... and our worst. I loathed the picture of myself that emerged when I expressed an impatient sigh, a bossy tone, or an irritated retort. And as the "good girl" image began to crumble, I felt guilty. Guilty for my lack of consistent support for the man God brought back to me. Guilty for my lapse of trust in the Lord's goodness and His promise of sufficient grace.

Even then, God repeatedly added quiet reassurances, sometimes through a kind word of a friend, a verse penned on a card, or the lyrics of a hymn. One day I happened to catch a radio speaker talk about the dangers of resentment and the importance of forgiveness. I jotted the notes into my journal.

Conversations with a counselor-friend also revealed my thinking patterns. I came to realize I am not responsible for the happiness of others. I do not have to mirror those around me, and I can be okay regardless of their ups and downs. "Every spouse fails," our friend further advised, "but instead of a cold shoulder or withdrawal, be ready with grace. Demonstrate kind consideration as Barry works through his issues, just as you want people to respect your pain and fears." He reminded me of the importance of mutual respect in any relationship.

Be ready with grace. Day after day I prayed I would stand by my husband, offering grace—and a safe place to heal.

More Physical Therapy

My daily pain colored my perceptions to a degree. As the first-year anniversary of the crash came and went, I still experienced significant stiffness. Some days I hurt all over. My shoulders ached something awful. When my parents took me to Johnstown for appointments, I could hardly manage the next day. My doctor finally sent me to a local neurosurgeon. He saw me for all of five minutes, if that. Then he handed me a script for more physical therapy.

Little did I know what a gift that little paper held. My therapist gave me a set of exercises—not hard and not long. In her wonderful, encouraging way, she taught me the correct way to do them. As the weeks went by, the pain subsided. By the time my visits expired with the insurance company, I felt like a new person. I faithfully worked out with the exercise ball, hand weights, and leg weights for weeks and months and years afterward. I still do. Not every day is pain-free, and I still have to "follow the rules," but, so far, I can do my daily work without regular pain meds.

Let's See What Daddy Thinks

As the months slipped by, I wanted to do everything I could to smooth out the wrinkles between Barry and the girls. Modeling acceptance and support became my first priority. As I journaled about my own frustrations and shortcomings, I found more room to accept Barry's limitations. I looked for ways to honor him, to thank him, and to adapt to him. Little by little, our marriage reflected a growing companionship.

I also made it a habit to say to five-year-old Elisabeth, "Let's see what Daddy thinks." Or, "Dad would know more about this subject. Let's ask him." It took a while, but Barry slowly won back her respect. He also became more involved in family discussions, times when we tried to work out differences and misunderstandings, especially with the older girls. I sometimes came away from these feeling like we had so far to go, but they represented a positive beginning.

Answered Prayers

As I prepared to write this book, I spent hours reading my journals from after the crash. I relived our story, full of miracles and setbacks, blessings and disappointments, victories and defeats. I tracked Barry's limitations and saw them lessen with each passing year. I noted my questions, many times recorded with few answers. I discovered nuggets of truth I had jotted down from God's Word that kept me going. I remembered the counsel we received that buoyed us up to a place of trust.

And I read my prayers ... broken, desperate prayers, written and offered to the only One who could truly help us. As I turned the pages, one after another, it dawned on me. *God answered my prayers.* When I look back on those days and compare them to the present, the faithfulness of God stands out boldly on every page.

Today, I treasure the memories of Jana's little boy, Ty, and his grandpa playing with blocks on the living room floor ... memories of Sharon's father walking her down the aisle on her wedding day and of the daddy-daughter dance at her reception ... of Elisabeth and her dad working on algebra and Latin together and chatting about sports and college and boys ... of daffodil and daisy bouquets on the dining room table from my man with the green thumb.

Jana and Sharon have become friends as they've grown older—supportive in many ways. Jana patiently helped me set up my blog. She connects with her dad about gardening and keeps in touch regularly. Sharon, now a nurse, offers positive insights and lends support in all things medical. Elisabeth blesses us by bringing humor, conversation, and friends to the dinner table. We're far from perfect, but when we gather together as a family, there's a warm feeling of loyalty, of belonging. We don't take it for granted. We know how much work it took to get here ... hard work wrapped up in grace. God's grace.

Acceptance and Commitment

Recently, a friend asked, "So, how are you and Barry doing? A lot of couples our age aren't doing so well."

In the seconds before I answered, I quietly rehearsed the journey Barry and I had traveled during these years. "We're doing fine now," I said.

But my perceptive friend, always able to draw people out, wanted more. "What's one thing that's helped you?" she pressed.

I didn't hesitate. "Acceptance."

She waited for me to continue.

"Barry and I need each other. Besides helping him with his limited vision, I bring balance to his responses. He enlarges my focus in areas of our finances, service to others, and parenting. He does the household tasks I find difficult like vacuuming, lifting, and yard work. We complement each other and depend on one another more than ever." Then I smiled. "He'd do *anything* for me."

Later, I reflected on the foundation of our relationship. Commitment. On July 14, 1979, amid flowers and tulle, we vowed "to have and to hold, from this day forward, for better, for worse, for richer, for poorer, in sickness and in health," to love each other "as long as we both shall live." We prayed that God would shepherd us, lead us, and "be the guardian of our way."[1] Our young idealism could never have imagined the future of our story, but God knew all along.

Like any couple, Barry and I have had differences and misunderstandings. But there's comfort in knowing the same grace that brought us through those early years after the crash will never run out. His grace—His favor, loving-kindness, and mercy—always matches the need. We can trust Him with our story "as long as we both shall live."

And beyond.

Annie Johnson Flint, confined to a wheelchair and in pain for many years, wrote poems and hymns attesting to God's love and grace. During these post-accident years, I've savored her reflections so vividly expressed:

> *He giveth more grace when the burdens grow greater,*
> *He sendeth more strength when the labors increase;*
> *To added affliction He addeth His mercy,*
> *To multiplied trials, His multiplied peace.*

When we have exhausted our store of endurance,
When our strength has failed ere the day is half done,
When we reach the end of our hoarded resources,
Our Father's full giving is only begun.

His love has no limits; His grace has no measure.
His power has no boundary known unto men;
For out of His infinite riches in Jesus,
He giveth, and giveth, and giveth again.[2]

CHAPTER SIXTEEN

No Other Plan?

THE COLLEGE PRESIDENT'S singular plan was to welcome Barry back to work, leading the academics of the college once again. Barry, himself, expected to return. I waived aside my initial doubts and hesitations. We never considered another option. The Office of Vocational Rehabilitation funded additional outpatient therapy at John Heinz with the goal of sending Barry back to work in a similar capacity. Day after day, he marched through his paces, recovering as many of his former abilities as possible.

In August, the president invited Barry to speak at convocation, a chapel service to initiate the fall semester. Barry wrote his thoughts out, and I typed them up. After a little wordsmithing, we printed his speech in a large font so he could see it better. I sat in the front row, still somewhat stiff, and proudly watched my husband, in his doctoral regalia, take his place at the podium. We celebrated a landmark victory that day complete with photos, handshakes, and hugs.

Barry's therapies finished on October 20, 2003, six months post-accident. With the assistance of the interim academic dean, he kept part-time office hours. He felt settled about returning to work but voiced his concerns: "Will I ever be close to what I was before?"

Soon, after practicing with me for weeks, Barry passed his driving test. His double vision affected his downward glance only, so he could see to drive. He also flew to Michigan to spend a few precious days with his dad who passed away later that fall.

Back to Work

In January 2004, just nine months after the crash, Barry went back to work full-time. A miracle. An answer to prayer. Back to normal. Finally.

But a brain stem injury and double vision don't heal like broken bones—good as new in six to eight weeks or even nine months. Again, we didn't know what we didn't know. In an effort to support Barry's return to work, his neuropsychologist recommended frequent evaluations of his performance.

Due to several transitions in personnel, Barry's responsibilities increased while his former coping skills decreased. He worked long hours, but a menacing shadow of frustration followed him. Often, he came home at lunchtime to catch a nap. His vision presented continual challenges. We both wondered if his position placed too much pressure on his shoulders.

Three long years later, in 2007, the college hired a new vice president in the academic area and named Barry as his assistant. Barry moved his office across the suite to a smaller space. Perhaps a position with diminished responsibilities would better fit his new normal, but besides the obvious adjustments, he didn't feel as needed in his new role.

By this time, both Barry and the college were weighing the option of long-term disability. In some areas, Barry continued to climb well past the two-year period of maximum recovery when he should have come to a plateau. However, the neuropsychologist reevaluated him several times over those years with little measurable change in other areas, casting more doubt on his ability to do his job. And his vision—always his double vision—made life difficult in every way.

In January 2008, four years after returning to work full-time, Barry agreed with the college's assessment that he could not fulfill his job responsibilities and, therefore, should pursue disability. His hours gradually decreased until his position was eliminated. By spring, he quietly packed up his office and relinquished his keys.

Our girls were upset. We all found ourselves wondering why Barry's efforts to go back to work had come to this. Now what? Again, I had to consider God's providence. God was bigger than this unexpected twist that turned "the plan" upside down. As in the past, He knew all about our needs, both material and immaterial.

Several months after leaving the college, we received Barry's first disability check with a built-in two-year provision for him to continue to seek a suitable job.

That same fall, he began teaching junior high history, literature, and Latin part-time in a small private school. He persevered through the end of the year, but when the alarm went off every morning, he all but begged God for strength, trying to gather up enough courage to face another day. He tutored some in the afternoons but always needed a midday rest.

More Adjustments

Gradually, it became clear Barry would not be able to maintain what the disability insurance company termed "similar work." But there was a tug-of-war in Barry's thinking. His work ethic and sense of responsibility clashed with his limitations. He wanted to contribute, not sit around the house, but what job would accommodate the repercussions of his injuries? My condition carried long-term restrictions too, and I felt committed to stay home with Elisabeth who had just turned ten.

Disability brought with it another set of adjustments. With time weighing heavy on his hands, Barry tried to fill his time constructively. Over the years, he has spent hours reviewing Latin, learning Spanish, and keeping up with Elisabeth in math. He never stopped gardening and tried various activities to determine what he might enjoy. Nevertheless, he often found himself restless. Sometimes he would wonder aloud, "Do I enjoy anything anymore?"

In His faithfulness, God gave Barry some wonderful opportunities to offer his talents in a variety of ways. He's led discussions on the classics at the local library, volunteered as a language coach, come alongside and encouraged young men with disabilities, served as a borough council member, and acted as an adviser and greeter at church. He's sat across the table from kids who needed help in math or Latin, often taking care to listen to them and see beyond that day's lesson to the whole person. Parents have told me numerous times of their appreciation for his focus and understanding—and his wise suggestions.

It hasn't always been easy to choose how and when to engage. Yet he has made many meaningful and constructive contributions to individuals and to the community. "Always for the other guy."[1] Always helping others find success.

Looking back, Barry always acknowledged God's hand in his disability status. "I couldn't do the job today. It's better this way."

I thanked God every month when the disability check arrived in our mailbox, even if it met our needs in a way we would not have chosen.

Broken Dreams

We had a good plan in place. One we all worked toward, especially Barry.

Sometimes, though, like an author's outline, the plot in our stories doesn't follow the direction we intended. We find ourselves in a different place, often with broken dreams at our feet. What then?

David, Israel's shepherd-king, experienced a similar disappointment. The same man who wrote, "As for God, his way is perfect; ... It is God who arms me with strength and makes my way perfect,"[2] had a great plan. He had it in his heart to build a temple for the Lord, a beautiful place of worship. Nathan the prophet told him, "Go ahead and do it, for the LORD is with you."[3] Even God said, "You did well to have this in your heart." But He went on to say, "Nevertheless, you are not the one to build the temple, but your son ... will build the temple for my Name."[4] David didn't meet the qualifications.

God doesn't judge us for our dreams. He sees beyond our intentions into our hearts. At times, He still says no. He redirects our steps and implements another plan.

David's response impresses me. He sat before the Lord and worshiped. "How great you are, O Sovereign LORD! There is no one like you ... Your words are trustworthy ..."[5]

Trustworthy. In author Kay Arthur's words, "Every disappointment is God's appointment."[6]

I wonder if David's son, Solomon, thought of his dad's desire to build the temple when he wrote these proverbs: "In his heart a man plans his course, but the LORD determines his steps.[7] Many are the plans in a man's heart, but it is the LORD'S purpose that prevails."[8]

God's plan for Barry did not pan out the way we prayed and hoped it would. It's a painful chapter of our story. He could not meet the expectations of others ... or himself. And yet, the goal of going back to his job gave him the tenacity to work hard. Perhaps if he had known the end of this chapter, he would never have reached his potential.

The Best Plan of All

About six years after my husband took on disability status, I stood in the kitchen peeling potatoes and happened to hear a radio interview with someone who graduated with Barry in 1983. At that time, they both received a Ph.D. Listening to the interview, I learned this man had spent over thirty years in higher education administration at three different Christian colleges and now worked with CEOs. I told Barry about it over dinner that night. We had lost touch with our friend and rejoiced to hear how the Lord had led him.

Later, I found myself musing over the contrast between the two men. Barry served as a teacher, a school principal, a college professor, and an administrator. He developed many programs and started a graduate school. But the car crash changed everything for him, and his story seemed to stop mid-paragraph. Despite his valiant efforts, only disconnected fragments now littered the next page.

Or did they?

A brighter picture emerged as I thought about the fact that every day I see a man who has become more patient. A man who remains faithful. And, according to the book of James, a man God considers blessed. "Blessed is the man who perseveres under trial, because when he has stood the test, he will receive the crown of life that God has promised to those who love him."[9] Barry's many—and often quiet—contributions come to mind. He's the guy who walks across the street to check on the neighbors and prays with them during the hard times. He's the church member who quietly slips a twenty-dollar bill to the visiting missionaries to make sure they have gas to get home. He brings his garden produce to the father of four who just received a pink slip. He shovels snow for an elderly neighbor who has no family. People describe him as gentle and kind ... honest, sincere, trustworthy ... a *good* man.

And every morning after the alarm goes off, he slips his arm around me and prays. I love to hear him pray. He thanks God for His greatness and how He has blessed us. He asks for wisdom, with reliance on a heavenly Father who cares for us, one day at a time.

I can't deny my spouse's different voice, but the driven man I once knew has become softer in many ways. More sensitive. Before the crash, Barry had more of a global influence. He helped organizations achieve their proper credentials and built programs to help students with an eye toward the future. Since the crash, he focuses on individuals and their needs with a personal interest, bringing each one closer to realizing his or her potential.

It's never easy to see those we love wrestle with limitations, struggle to find purpose, and feel restless. Yet Barry has pursued faithfulness and fruitfulness in whatever opportunities God has brought his way. In the years following the crash, he still aims to exemplify lifelong learning alongside a love for God and others.

It's been said that hard times can make a person bitter or better. Despite Barry's staggering losses, I realize that I don't live with a man who exemplifies bitterness. In my estimation, he is choosing, with God's help, to allow his new normal to make him better.

The best plan of all.

Your Story

At times, God may redirect your steps and implement another plan. Give an example from your life story that illustrates how God changed your plan. Remember a time when pain, fear, or frustration gave way to anger. Consider specific ways to offer grace and respect to those with differences or disabilities. What is the role of acceptance in a relationship? Based on chapters fifteen and sixteen, list some specific answers to your broken prayers and dreams. Write a prayer or story of trust. Refer to 1 Chronicles 17:1-15; Proverbs 16:9; 19:21; and James 1:12.

PART FOUR

PIECES OF THE MOSAIC

CHAPTER SEVENTEEN

The Place of Compliance

THE PASSING OF years brings perspective to any story. Ours is no exception. Looking back, we seek to understand how this specific chapter fits with the others in our lives. We want to remember what we learned as we walk into the future.

The place of compliance, a significant theme in my own personal story, illustrates one such lesson. Pictures of my compliant childhood followed me into adulthood. God blesses obedience and respect for authority, but can one exercise too much compliance? Too much deference? Too much acquiescence? I never considered these questions until a string of events brought them up close and personal. I recorded my journey in the form of an allegory.

Early on, Compliance became my friend.

In my growing-up years, Compliance showered me with many favors and benefits. She had a knack for keeping me out of trouble. She counseled me to listen to my parents and teachers. She encouraged me to memorize Scripture, serve in the church, and attend a Christian college to prepare for ministry. She drew me into wholesome activities and walked me down the aisle in a pure white dress. With Compliance by my side, rules and guidelines didn't bother me much. To this point, I trusted most of the authorities in my life. Some forty years later, I still feel grateful for their protection. I avoided many typical pitfalls and upheld moral values and ideals. For the most part, the pages of my story remained clean and unsullied.

I have to fess up to a seventh-grade lapse when I snuck off and left Compliance standing alone and abandoned. After about three months, I decided it wasn't worth it. Who wants conflict all the time? It wasn't fun playing tug-of-war with my dad and mom. And so, with Determination cheering me on, I sprinted back to where I'd left my friend. She saw me coming, and her warm, safe smile of approval welcomed me back. This time, I clung to her tighter than ever. I would try to do everything *right*. No questions asked.

As the years slipped by, I drew near to God by reading His Word and reaching for the standards I had been taught. Life seemed black and white then. Soon enough, tentacles of gray began to steal around the edges of my story. Holding the hand of Compliance alone could not equip me to navigate the somber chapters ahead.

It all began with my children. I introduced them to Compliance and encouraged them to befriend her. But one of them wasn't so sure she wanted to buddy-up with this straight-laced companion of mine. And she didn't mind playing tug-of-war with me either. I didn't understand her. What was she thinking?

For the first time, my world rocked and rolled. I knew no other way to do life. I fell to my knees and cried out for help. The Lord, ever-present to the brokenhearted, gave me hope bit by tiny bit. But it took time before I fully embraced the concept that befriending Compliance is not the same as drawing near to God with my *heart*. Only He can make me righteous—not my efforts to be the good girl by complying with a set of standards.

God still had more to teach me about the proper place of Compliance. The next unforgettable lesson came just days after the car crash. I lay in traction awaiting surgery. When the recommendation came from one of Barry's doctors to stop the respirator, I never questioned it. He offered no hope that my husband would pull through. An expert had spoken.

It didn't occur to me that it had been only a few days since the foggy pile-up, the diagnosis, the coma. I never thought about the fact that I hadn't had a chance to thoroughly understand his prognosis, ask for a second opinion—or even see him. The potential for loss was staggering—for me, our three girls, and so many others. Compliance dictated my response, as she had done for so many years. I did what I was told. I didn't consider another option.

What was *I* thinking?

When my mom brought Inquiry to my hospital room, I reached for this friendship with an eager hand. In the weeks and months that followed, I also enlisted the help of Reason, Perception, and Discernment. As much as I still appreciated Compliance, I needed a multitude of counselors to help me *think*, not just follow. I prayed earnestly, begging God to also send Wisdom to help me.

Beyond Compliance

Trauma never leaves you the same. Our accident acted as a catalyst for many long-term changes. Since that pivotal life-or-death decision for Barry, I'm learning to know the Lord for His blessings and guidance—and also for Himself. I want to ask appropriate questions, questions that play a significant role in navigating life's dilemmas with God's direction. I desire to draw near to Him with my heart rather than my list.

With our daughters, I hope to actively listen, see past the surface, and focus on what's truly important in the light of all eternity. I want to model compliance and obedience to God, yes, but in addition, employ multiple tools to critically evaluate all that comes along. It's a lifelong process as we help each other claim the treasure of an inner soul connection to God.

Since our older girls have about eleven and fourteen years on the last one, I often hear comments about how my parenting has softened. I overheard the oldest remark to the youngest, "When *we* were teenagers, Mom would have a cow. Now she only has a calf!" All those years of struggle wrapped up in one astute observation. Her comment made me smile.

Nurturing Compliant Voices

Perhaps not everyone can identify with being too compliant. Perhaps there's a need for some to befriend Compliance to a greater extent. Both ends of the continuum need to seek a healthy balance.

As I've contemplated this characteristic, I've noticed traits we compliants have in common. We're the *nice* people who make it a pattern to defer to others. We have few opinions of our own. We can rarely identify our feelings, let alone put them into words. We grew up "the good kids" who seldom crossed an authority figure. We do what we're told without question. We feel intimidated by those with strong opinions and can easily be manipulated. Sometimes these qualities—even the positive ones—get us into trouble.

I know. I almost pulled the plug on my husband—because a specialist said so—without asking one single question.

Obedience and compliance are important. Training children to obey our voice protects them from harm. Willingness to yield[1] oils our relationships. God-given authorities offer us a shield of protection. Seeking counsel symbolizes humility and a teachable spirit. But when we inadvertently absolve ourselves of the responsibility to think, to ask questions, and to act in our personal best interest, we end up pleasing people instead of pleasing God.

As I worked through my own imbalance in this area, I recognized some of these same tendencies in Sharon. I didn't want her to be taken advantage of, to always find herself at the end of the line, to struggle to form and stick to her own opinions. I wanted her to have a voice.

Through the rest of high school and her first couple years of college, I encouraged her to ask more questions. To act based on conviction—not because someone said so—and to stand up for herself. She's still sweet as ever, but her voice leans well to the side of strength and balance.

I'm finding that part of trusting God with our stories involves taking responsibility for our lives. We are responsible in matters related to everything from medical decisions to food choices. It's prudent to ask questions. It's wise to postpone a decision until we have the information we need.

Before the crash, I didn't have much of a voice. Out of necessity, it has become stronger, but I still struggle to strike a balance. Compliance has its place. Yet, as I discovered, there's more. Much more. We possess the ability to choose to surround ourselves with the necessary tools to evaluate our circumstances and make constructive decisions. We can make it a point to nurture the voices of others. After all, the compliant among us also have a significant story.

> Whoever is simple (easily led astray and wavering), let
> him turn in here! As for him who lacks understanding,

[God's] Wisdom says to him, Come, eat of my bread
... And walk in the way of insight *and* understanding.[2]
The prudent man looks and considers well where he
is going.[3]

Your Story

An unhealthy balance in the area of compliance brings us to
the point of pleasing people instead of pleasing God. Where on
the compliance continuum do you find yourself? List dangers
present at either extreme. In which areas do you need to
become more willing to yield? In which areas do you need to ask
questions and become more responsible? How can you cultivate
the voice of another? Meditate on the concepts presented in
chapter 17 and write a prayer or story of trust. Refer to Proverbs
9:4-6; 14:15; Ephesians 5:15-21; and James 3:13-18.

CHAPTER EIGHTEEN

Victim or Victor?

I MADE UP my mind. Regardless of my lifelong limitations, I made a decision. *I am not the victim anymore.*

Victim had been my name long enough.

The turnpike pileup inflicted injuries that required extensive surgeries, therapies, and adjustments. I had been wounded and vulnerable, dependent on family, friends, and modern medicine to do *everything* for me. I couldn't help but play the role of victim for months. One Sunday morning, however, I determined that the crash would not be my permanent identity.

The Victim

After the shocking news of our trauma, life moved on for the people around us while we found ourselves bound to hospital beds, rehab centers, and therapy routines. When we needed help after coming home, the kindnesses of many touched us deeply. Thoughtful people often asked, "How are you doing?" all the while shaking their heads in an affirmative direction. They had invested time in prayer and countless other benevolences. We *must* be improving, but not always. How could I disappoint them with a less than positive response?

Even after my injuries healed and I could function in a somewhat normal capacity, the label of "accident victim" seemed to be written across my forehead. And perhaps, more than I wanted to admit, this same identity colored my outlook. Trapped by our daily limitations, Barry and I grieved our losses and all that had happened to us. We struggled to accept the no-turning-back changes we experienced.

Connecting with others on another level beyond our

circumstances left me impatient and frustrated as I tried to overcome the victim status. That morning in the church hallway, after mulling it over for weeks, I concluded that only one person could change my victim mindset.

Me.

I had choices. My tragedy did not make me a pawn on the great chessboard of life. I could initiate concern about the joys and problems of others. I could take responsibility for my thinking and move on. In God's providence, the car crash would affect the rest of my story every single day, but it didn't have to define me. If I wanted to move from victim to victor, *I* had to make the change.

The Mosaic

We've all been victims to varying degrees. Every one of us has been hurt, wounded, or adversely affected by something or someone. We've all experienced loss. How easy to feel stuck in these vulnerable places—angry, frustrated, consumed, powerless. To feel as if we have few choices and can't move past what has happened to us. God understands our pain. He sympathizes "with our weaknesses" and "has been tempted in every way, just as we are ..."[1]

During the weeks and months of our recovery and beyond, I found solace in the listening ear of God and in jotting down my thoughts, feelings, and prayers. I tried to remind myself of truth even when it seemed counterintuitive.

How essential for me to remember the place of providence in my story. To remember that God writes perfect stories in which He promises His precious presence. To remember He always has a purpose for what He allows into my life, even when that purpose seems cloudy to me. Seeing my pain through God's all-knowing point of view brought me back to His piercing question, "Will you trust Me?"

Perhaps, like me, you've found that moving beyond the victim mindset takes time. At the height of my pain, every fiber in me wanted to scream, "No! Why did this happen to *me*? To *us*?" As I processed my grief, I gradually let go of allowing my pain to define me. I started to look forward. God took my woundedness, paired it with His grace, and placed them into the mosaic of my backstory. The dark shades of my pain and the light hues of His grace, side by side, display an image ... a picture of hope.

And sometimes—when others who are hurting and broken see this picture—our common experience births a sweet connection between us. Together, we "approach the throne of grace with confidence, so that we may receive mercy and find grace to help us in our time of need."[2] Together, we consider our place in God's epic story. Together, we reflect on the good that can grow out of our heartaches, benefits we didn't expect: compassion, patience, sensitivity, trust.

This picture brings to mind the apostle Paul's words to the Corinthian believers: "Praise be to ... the Father of compassion and the God of all comfort, who comforts us in all our troubles, so that we can comfort those in any trouble with the comfort we ourselves have received from God."[3]

Comfort from God, Himself. Personal comfort. He consoles and encourages us in every trouble, calamity, and affliction of our earthbound stories.[4] We, in turn, comfort others.

After the crash, my identity was wrapped up in the trauma, our healing journey, family struggles, our limitations, and my role while Barry worked his way back from the coma. In His trustworthiness, God tenderly picked me up. He brushed the dirt away and poured the oil of His love on my wounds. He steadied me and walked forward with me.

He redefined me ... a victor.

Do You Want To Get Well?

Jesus once crossed paths with a man who had been an invalid for thirty-eight long years—thirty-eight years of lying on a woven mat, unable to walk. No cure. Little hope. Did an accident cancel his former life? Did his friends drop off, one by one? Did he beg in the streets for a bit of bread? Jesus paused, singled him out among the others with disabilities, and looked him in the eye. "Do you want to get well?"[5] An odd question for a man who'd been sick for so long.

But perhaps not so peculiar. Victims identify with their pain after a while. It's comfortable. Predictable. Even beneficial. To become other than the victim poses unknown possibilities and increased expectations. And what about the risk?

At first, change feels clumsy. It costs something.

The man with a mat shared his story with Jesus. And when Jesus commanded, "Get up! Pick up your mat and walk,"[6] he wasted no time doing just that.

This reminds me of our neighbor. User of a wheelchair since birth, he has limited use of his limbs. Every day presents a challenge. Helpers come and go, but no one would say he's the victim. He goes to work and to the mall on the bus, takes "walks" up and down the streets, serves on the town council, and even lives alone. He always has a smile and a positive word. Somewhere in his story, he made a conscious decision to "get up."

There's no magic formula to move beyond the emotions of helplessness, blame, self-pity, or the grieving process. So much rests in the way one thinks and believes. It's seldom easy. In the end, if one wants to get well, one must be willing to "get up."

We may need a hand from a willing helper. We may need time to get our bearings. We may need to take baby steps. But with God at our side, we can move forward with grace.

Finding the Balance

In time, I turned a corner. My conversations focused more on others and their needs. I purposed to thank God for what I *could* do. Gradually, I started to see myself differently. Limited, yes, but with the ability to choose, to do my work in other ways.

I weed my flower beds by getting down on all fours instead of squatting and bending over. I carry lighter bags of groceries from the car into the house and routinely ask for help to lug the vacuum upstairs or set my sewing machine on the table. Someone else places my grandchildren on my lap, or I get down on the floor to play with them. I have discovered how to do daily tasks in new ways.

Sometimes in my effort to escape the victim mentality, I have swung over to the other side of the pendulum, the side that touches on denial. Feeling fine most days, after all, I could ignore the pain—to a point. I shrank away from one more doctor telling me what could go wrong. Wanting to get on with my life, I kept up with my exercise routine and maintained a healthy lifestyle but for several years could not bring myself to see my primary care physician for so much as a script for routine blood work.

Ignoring problems doesn't make them go away. Part of wellness embraces a realistic outlook. I'm aiming to achieve balance. Not a victim. Not in denial. When I reached the age when restaurants give the senior discount, I took a deep breath, squared my shoulders, and made a few doctor's appointments.

Victim or victor? Acknowledging our pain and realistically working through our grief leads to healing and trust. "Now thanks be to God who always leads us in triumph in Christ, and through us diffuses the fragrance of His knowledge in every place."[7]

Your Story

Your pain affects the rest of your story every day, but it does not need to define you. Describe one experience that has left you a victim. How does trust in God and His providence help you work through the grieving process? Do you want to get well? What will it mean for you to "get up" and move beyond victim to victor? How can you avoid denial? How can you represent God to others in their healing? Reflect on the principles in chapter 18 and write a prayer or story of trust. Consider John 5:1-15; 2 Corinthians 1:3, 4; 2:14; Hebrews 4:14-16.

CHAPTER NINETEEN

Trusting God to Write Your Story

I HAVE WITNESSED miracle after miracle since the crash on April 5, 2003. I experienced healing, benefited from the compassion of family and community, and accepted our new normal. I endeavored to find the place of compliance and rise above the victim mindset. With an often wavering yet sincere focus, I embraced the wisdom of trusting my heavenly Father who writes my story with love and grace.

But sometimes ... I'm afraid.

I suppose many emotions surface in the aftermath of a tragedy like ours: anger, resentment, blame, frustration, sadness, depression, and hopelessness. But for me, I struggle the most with fear.

From my childhood, fear troubled me. I remember my mom leaving a note on the kitchen table after school: *At the store. Be back soon. Psalm 56:3.* She had shared this Scripture with me many times. I knew it by heart: "What time I am afraid, I will trust in thee."[1] As a teen, I underlined 2 Timothy 1:7 in my Bible: "For God has not given us a spirit of fear, but of power and of love and of a sound mind."[2]

Our crash gave fear a new definition.

Anything to do with driving or riding in a car still puts knots in my stomach. Rain, fog, and snow double my anxiety. All these years later, bad weather on the road brings me right back to that foggy spring morning.

I know what can happen.

God finds us where we are. He offers specific Scriptures to meet our specific needs. He comforts us when we're afraid. I treasure His intentional yet tender touches of truth, clear snapshots that offer me assurance and hope.

Hemmed In

Our two older girls now live on the other end of a stretch of interstate known for frequent fog. A desire to visit them plays tug-of-war with my fears and apprehensions.

On one particular late fall day, a good weather report put my mind at ease as I headed south to see Sharon. However, an hour into my trip, clear visibility gave way to the dreaded dense fog. I gripped the wheel tighter and prayed for grace. Travel still acted as a trigger for me. After the car crash, I begged God for a promise that He would keep further trauma at bay. He gently showed me that trust does not insist on a perpetual safety guarantee and ideal outcomes. Rather, trust is resting in the One who always does what is best and brings glory to Himself.

Straining to see, I hoped I was trusting.

Earlier that morning, I had decided to play a Scripture CD in the car. The words of the Psalms calmed my rising uneasiness. I clicked on my flashers and lowered my speed to where I could stop within the length of my vision. Cars passed me, some without lights, and disappeared into the eerie whiteness ahead. I wished I could follow someone at a safe distance, but for miles I virtually drove alone on this venture gone south. Finally, a car with flashers followed behind me. I somehow felt safer—until he exited into opaque oblivion.

An hour later, the fog gradually dissipated. I breathed a sigh of relief. I don't know how many times the CD of verses repeated itself, but suddenly familiar words caught my attention. Words that became personal. "You hem me in—behind and before; you have laid your hand upon me."[3] God, with His all-powerful hand, hemmed me in every mile I drove in the fog. Like escort vehicles in front of and behind an oversized load, His presence surrounded me. I had to consider that His grace surrounds us *all* the time—when we arrive at our destination safely and even when we do not. I remember this promise every time I buckle up for a road trip—a conscious resolution to trust Him.

Backseat Driver

Just before the beginning of her junior year of high school, Elisabeth came home with a shiny new driver's license in her hand and a smile on her face. She passed the test after the required sixty-five plus hours of practice. Tears came to my eyes as I gave her a congratulatory hug. Her license represented not only a victory for her but also for me.

The prospect of coaching a new driver caused me more apprehension than I'd like to admit. Not that she drove differently from any other learner. Aside from a few mishaps early on, she did quite well, yet I didn't anticipate how difficult this would be for me. I had to make a conscious choice to accept my responsibility to help her reach this milestone.

During the summer leading up to her test—on our annual pilgrimage to Michigan—I spent many hours in the backseat with sixteen-year-old Elisabeth at the wheel. Barry coached her from the front passenger seat. There's something unnerving about the backseat. I couldn't see much, but sometimes what I *could* see resulted in giving my two cents—*not* a great idea.

One night, as Elisabeth cruised along the freeway, I felt on edge in my backseat position. As darkness fell, I prayed for peace and safety but couldn't shake the feeling. Finally, I turned on my Kindle and found my place in Grace L. Fabian's book, *Outrageous Grace: A Story of Tragedy and Forgiveness.* A couple pages in, I read, "I knew whatever happened, it was God who had the final say. Prayers ascended. It's okay to be in the dark with God. His presence makes all the difference."[4]

These words relayed Grace's trust when she didn't know if she would live or die due to medical complications. She lay stretched out in the back of a van while the driver navigated seventy-five miles of dark, windy, pot-holed New Guinea roads through the rain and fog to get to the nearest hospital.

Sometimes a story gives perspective. It quiets fears that hover in the shadows. I will never forget God's reassurance to me in the backseat that night.

A Role Model to Follow

The testimonies and victories of others press courage into our hearts when we're afraid. The biblical character, Sarah, has a story that strengthens me in the seeming merry-go-round of life. She had every reason to feel frightened.

Without warning, God spoke to her husband, Abraham, in the ancient land of Mesopotamia. "Leave your country, your people and your father's household, and go to the land I will show you."[5] The ultimate road trip for that place in time. How did Sarah respond to the news? Did she pack her household goods with an air of excitement, the promise of blessing making her mind race with possibilities? Did doubts steal into her dreams in the quiet of the night? Did she regret trading her wealthy surroundings and lifestyle for a caravan traveling hundreds of slow miles with campouts night after night to ... where?

And what about the times her husband schemed to save his skin by claiming Sarah as his sister? How did she feel when taken into the harems of not one, but two powerful rulers? Then after God's promise of a child, years of waiting slipped into decades. Did she fear she would never hold a tiny bundle in her arms?

Near the end of the New Testament, the apostle Peter paints a portrait of a woman with "the unfading beauty of a gentle and quiet spirit, which is of great worth in God's sight."[6] Tucked in his short discourse, he mentions Sarah as an example of a wife who followed her husband, yes, but greater than that, she trusted in God. "You are her daughters if you do what is right and do not give way to fear."[7]

Do what is right. Do not give way to fear. Time and time again I have clung to these words. *The Amplified Bible* translates it: "Let nothing terrify you [not giving way to hysterical fears or letting anxieties unnerve you]."[8] Sarah followed her husband. She acknowledged his headship. She called him lord. She must have loved him, but she trusted God.

I'm finding the antidote for fear. It's trust.

We all grapple with fear-based what ifs. Yet the same trustworthy God of Sarah walks with us. He writes our stories, penned without ink, fitting all things into a plan for good.[9] He always leads us in the paths of righteousness.[10] Trust follows Sarah's example: *Do what is right. Do not give way to fear.*

A Promise for Each Day

In the early weeks of my recovery, facing a new day of challenges seemed daunting to me. Meditation on specific Scriptures served as a practical way to face my fears. Rehearsing Isaiah 41:10 became a habit I still practice every morning. Slowly, I meditate on each phrase of a promise first relayed by a prophet to Israel centuries after God's first instructions to Abraham. "So do not fear, for I am with you; do not be dismayed, for I am your God. I will strengthen you and help you; I will uphold you with my righteous right hand."

God understands our residual emotions after a traumatic event. He offers personal comfort and hope through His Word. Every day He promises His presence and upholds us with His hand. We can trust Him.

Your Story

The antidote for fear is trust. What emotional residue lingers from a traumatic experience in your life? Choose one emotion with which you struggle. Link specific Scriptures to your feelings, visualizing God's truth in your situation. What does it mean for you to trust God with your story, both past and present? What lessons can you draw from Sarah's life? Reflecting on chapter 19, write a prayer or story of trust. Refer to Genesis 12; Psalm 56:3; 139:5; Isaiah 41:10; and 1 Peter 3:1-6.

CHAPTER TWENTY

The Rest of the Story

I CHERISH THE memories of cozy times with our little girls, still damp from a bath, cuddled close in their jammies. After the last "happily ever after," I tucked each one into bed with a prayer and a kiss. There's something compelling about the simple resolution of a story.

Our accident story's resolution is not so simple. Nonetheless, now that the plot has all but come to rest, I'm drawn to consider the present and the future through the grid of the past.

It's been over a dozen years since the pile-up in the fog in 2003. Time has brought change to the main characters in our story.

Jana finished college with a degree in art history. Over the years, she has contributed her skills and demonstrated her capabilities in a variety of ways, including freelance editing and website design. I value her contributions to this book. As the family computer expert, she willingly looks over Word documents and résumés, helps us with technology purchases, and makes it all look easy. I treasure our frequent phone conversations. Jana's young son, Ty, is all boy. He likes to dig, romp, jump, and ride his bike. He enjoys school—and he loves a story.

At times I've wondered if Sharon would have survived the crash had she been sitting in her usual place in the backseat of the car on that fateful day. She didn't want to leave home for college with all we'd been through together. After attending our local Penn State campus, she passed her boards to become a registered nurse. She brought a deep well of compassion to her patients in one of our area hospitals. After her wedding in 2012, she went to work for a same-day surgery center, the area of nursing she likes best. Sharon and her husband have become the proud parents of a little boy named William. I always appreciate our good talks.

Jana and Sharon, with their families, live about three hours from us—and only twenty minutes from each other. Even with the distance, we intentionally keep in touch and visit when we can. I love it when we're all together.

The little girl with two black eyes has grown up. While wearing my halo, I begged God to allow me to heal enough to be a good mother to her. I don't take it for granted. Elisabeth has a goal of someday working for a non-profit organization. She studies hard and plays the piano and keyboard. During high school, she spent a summer in South Africa working with disadvantaged children at Dayspring Children's Village. These experiences have contributed to her global perspective and her heart for those in need.

My parents continued to lend their faithful support during our post-trauma years. In the fall of 2011, my mom received the diagnosis of ovarian cancer. It became our turn to care for her and support my dad. Surgeries, chemo treatments, and strokes culminated in her death in August 2013. Mom's faith—the same faith that upheld us during our crisis—carried her to her last breath. She gave me countless gifts. I miss her.

Two months after Mom passed away, Dad underwent triple bypass surgery. Time and grace have brought him back to swimming three times a week, honing his art talent, and serving in his church. He comes for supper every Tuesday, and I pop in to see him once or twice a week. He's an integral part of our family.

My sister, Barb, and her husband live in Indiana now. Official empty nesters, they've become grandparents too. Barb and I live ten hours apart, but we've grown closer over the past few years. She's become my confidant and prayer partner—a true sister and friend.

Barry's family still makes Michigan their home. Every summer we buckle up and make the fourteen-hour drive to spend a few days together at Maxine and Ernie's cottage on Lake Michigan "up north." Not long after helping us, Barry's brother and sister-in-law, Gary and Karen, adopted a baby named Grace, now little sister to their two adult children. Barry's niece, Rayan, and her husband, Peter, have three little ones. There's more to our vacation than rolling waves, dune grass, and burgers on the grill. Every time the family gathers, there's the feeling of belonging, cherished by us all.

And what about Barry and me? We live in the same white house with the white picket fence and red door. We lead quiet lives peppered with community, family, and service. Our goal remains the same: to love God and love our neighbors. I savor the gift of every day.

Sometimes we enjoy idyllic days but, like most people, not often enough. Not only do we live in a fallen world, but illness and disappointment strike, challenges of our children and others concern us, and we sense our vulnerability with the passing of time.

As I write this last chapter, Barry finds himself struggling with the aftermath of an unexpected surgery. He's exhausted, in pain, and can't keep much down. I've taken him to the ER twice and to the doctor twice. Something's not right. I realize more than ever how much he usually contributes to our little household. In time, I expect he'll find his way back. But today? Uncertainties plague me. Unknowns surround me.

All over again, it's a matter of trust. Trusting God to write *this* chapter of our story.

Recently, I asked my sister, "How about this title for my next book ... *In Over My Head?*" We laughed together, but I feel that way a lot lately. And if I do write about this topic, the themes of trust and hope will likely stand out boldly on the page—both vivid pictures of how God's story interlinks with mine.

A Faithful Finish

As I live out the timeline of my life story, I carry with me an indelible desire to finish well. When I read or hear of those who began with high ideals, lived their dreams, overcame obstacles, helped humanity, and then botched it at the end, it scares me.

People seldom intend a negative outcome. Not long ago, I flipped through my Bible and identified characters who led exemplary lives at the start but whose storylines unraveled by the end. Rebekah traveled 500 miles by camel to become Isaac's bride then played favorites against her husband, deceiving him in his old age. Saul, Israel's first king, stood head and shoulders above the people but died in battle because of his rationalized disobedience. Judas, one of Jesus' closest associates, betrayed Him for a mere thirty pieces of silver. Sad stories, yet not far removed from the twenty-first century.

Who among us is exempt from slipping away from all we hold dear? How easy to let the slow leaks of sin deflate our spiritual momentum and godly intentions. One poor choice leads to another and before we know it, we have trivialized God's Word, grabbed the pencil, and scrawled an alternate plot.

Other biblical personalities modeled faithfulness in the closing chapters of their lives. Ruth remained loyal to her mother-in-law and adopted the God of Israel. At the end of Paul's life, he claimed, "I have finished the race, I have kept the faith."[1] I'm intrigued with the apostle John who became a writer in his sunset years. He penned a biography of Jesus, three letters, and in his nineties, the epic book of Revelation. These saints experienced lapses of faith here and there, but they gripped the grab bar of truth, found their bearings once again, and marched forward, true to the end.

Finishing well starts with the present. As God writes my story, He promises to walk close beside me to the last word of the last paragraph of the last page of my life ... and beyond. From my vantage point, I navigate an unknown future but not without known truth. His promises never expire ... all the way to the end.

The Best is Yet to Come

Heaven represents a bit of a mystery to me. The last book of the Bible cites many other-worldly sights: gates made of pearls, a golden street, colorful precious stones, white robes, angels, a sea of glass like crystal, and the tree of life. Hard for me to imagine.

I'm drawn most to what will *not* be there. The apostles recorded, "[God] will wipe every tear from their eyes. There will be no more death or mourning or crying or pain, for the old order of things has passed away."[2] Our inheritance "can never perish, spoil or fade."[3] The concept of night will vanish. "They will not need the light of a lamp or the light of the sun, for the Lord God will give them light."[4] Impurity will never "enter [the city] ... but only those whose names are written in the Lamb's book of life."[5]

All the challenges of this life will fade away. All the mortal hurt and confusion and tears and darkness. Every sin and act of prejudice and injustice. And ... all the human experiences of the car crash. There's hope in these Scriptures, and in the fact that "the throne of God and of the Lamb (Jesus) will be in the city, and ... they will see his face ..."[6] This is the best part of our future story.

Trusting God to Write Your Story

C. S. Lewis wrote, "If you read history you will find that the Christians who did most for the present world were just those who thought most of the next ... Aim at Heaven and you will get earth 'thrown in': aim at earth and you will get neither."[7] Perhaps the heroes of faith in Hebrews 11 carried this out best. "They admitted that they were aliens and strangers on earth. ... They were longing for a better country—a heavenly one."[8]

My paternal grandmother, born in 1904, lived with her focus on eternity. I loved the family spaghetti dinners at her and Grandpa's home with all the relatives. But her faith over many years made the deepest impression on me.

In the weeks before she passed away, she said with confidence, "I hear the singing. Don't you hear them singing?" In the quiet of her room, did she hear the music of heaven? The praise of white-robed angels and saints? Her last words demonstrated a holy eagerness to enter her heavenly Father's house. "Open the gates! Open the gates!"

I can't help but think that when her earthly story ended, the shining ones led her by the hand, and the gates of pearl swung open. The brightness of God's glory enveloped her as the music swelled to receive her into the very presence of the Lord. "Welcome home, Matilda. Welcome home."

A happily-ever-after story.

How would our daily lives change if we lived in the reality of what we possess? If we heard the singing? If we caught a glimpse of heaven's gates? If we aimed at heaven in every line of our life stories, penned without ink?

For me, it all crescendos toward trust. Trust in the God who desires to write every detail of my earthbound story. As

He walks beside me, He always has my best interests in mind. He journeys with me all the way to the last page and beyond. He's worthy of my every confidence ... even in the aftermath of a foggy crash on the Pennsylvania Turnpike.

Today, He asks, "Will you trust Me? Will you place a white rose of surrender at the foot of the cross?"

Today I ask, "Will you trust God to write *your* story?"

Your Story

Finishing well starts with the present. How does the passing of time give your story perspective? What strategies or routines do you have in place to finish well? Which description of heaven most appeals to you? How would your life change if you made it a priority to aim at heaven? For what experience or circumstance do you need to trust God the most? Will you trust God with your story? Based on chapter 20, write a prayer or story of trust. Meditate on 2 Timothy 4:7; Hebrews 11:13-16; and Revelation 21 and 22.

EPILOGUE

An Unforeseen Chapter

IT'S BEEN THIRTEEN years since the car crash and nearly a year since I finished writing our story. I will always cherish the memories of Barry sitting with me at the kitchen table at lunchtime while I read each finished chapter to him. He often offered suggestions, especially with regard to his journey in Chapter 16. I came to appreciate and depend on his input. When I completed the last chapter, he wasn't feeling well, yet he patiently listened to each word from his recliner. I had little reason to believe this would be the last time we would review my writing together.

Less than a week after we went over those last few pages, emergency room visits, appointments with doctors, and my best nursing efforts ended with a call to 911. Three days later, with our family gathered around him in the ICU, Barry passed on into the arms of the One he so faithfully served. No more double vision. No more limitations. He fought the good fight. He finished the race. He kept the faith (2 Timothy 4:7).

But his passing also left our daughters fatherless, our grandsons missing their grandpa, and his siblings lacking their brother. His death left his students without a tutor, our church without a friendly greeter, the pastoral staff without a consultant, the borough without a council member, and his friends without the companion they loved and respected.

And with little warning, I became a widow.

In the midst of my grief and the endless necessary paperwork, Lighthouse Publishing of the Carolinas offered me a book contract. A light in the darkness. A new opportunity. The next thing. As I polished my manuscript yet one more time, the comfort and hope I wrote about once again began to shine healing into my aching heart. Even with this latest blow, the truths I myself had written within these pages rang true. As I've tried to sort it all out, I've been drawn to trust the Master Writer at an even deeper level.

Because I finished writing the book while Barry was still with us, I've left the most recent parts in present tense. It seems to me the best way to tell the story.

May I leave you with one final thought—one that has been a lifeline for me over the past weeks and months? Perhaps it will encourage you too.

One morning, a little phrase from the book of Hebrews leaped off the page. "Let us run with perseverance the race marked out for us" (Hebrews 12:1). These words reminded me of Elisabeth's experience running cross country. The course, marked out ahead of time and made visible by spray-painted arrows in the path, indicated the trail the runners were to follow.

Reading this verse, it occurred to me anew that our race has been planned out for us by our loving heavenly Father. The race marked out for *me* includes becoming a widow. It means times of tears, regret, and lonely emptiness. It means learning what to do when the *good* car breaks down, when the crawlspace is taking on water, and when I have to figure out the finances. It means making decisions on my own, carrying the concerns of my children without Barry's insights, and asking for help—again. It means learning to enjoy life once more and looking for new ways to serve. I want to run with perseverance, with intention, rather than give up because my partner no longer runs by my side. How essential to remember God's care and lovingkindness … to trust Him.

Before Elisabeth's races, the athletes would walk the course ahead of time to become familiar with the route. In life, we can't look into the future. But Jesus Himself has walked this path before us. He knows the way. So whether we're sprinting up a hill, watching for knotted roots in the woods, or slogging down a muddy embankment, He's been there ahead of us. He promises never to leave or forsake us (Hebrews 13:5, 6).

I find myself asking the same questions in my journal as I did after the car crash: What does faithfulness look like now?

What is the will of God for me today? And again, God's Word strengthens me, giving me the courage and grit to move forward: For you have need of steadfast patience *and* endurance, so that you may perform *and* fully accomplish the will of God, ... We are of those who believe [who cleave to and trust in and rely on God through Jesus Christ, the Messiah] *and* by faith preserve the soul" (Hebrews 10:36, 39 AMP).

As you and I entrust our life stories to God's capable pen, I pray we will draw ever closer to Him and trust Him in *every* situation ... all the way to the end.

May the God of hope
fill you with all joy and peace
as you trust in him,
so that you may overflow with hope
by the power of the Holy Spirit.

Romans 15:13

To view photos of our story, visit www.PennedWithoutInk.com.

THANK YOU ...

To Eddie Jones, Cindy Sproles, Andrea Merrell, and the wonderful team at Lighthouse Publishing of the Carolinas, who patiently mentored me and shared my vision for this story.

To those who willingly gave of their time to write an endorsement, to be an influencer, and to double-check every word, punctuation mark, and reference.

To the prayer warriors who believed in this project over several years, including those who faithfully study God's Word and pray at Kim Gromacki's home on Wednesday evenings.

To those who graciously allowed me to share their stories within these pages.

To my loyal writer friends who always ask the right questions, push me past the expected, cheer me on ... and read innumerable rewrites: Sherry Boykin, Leslee Clapp, Barbara Engle, Gail Mills, Rebecca Loescher, Cindy Noonan, and Jo Ann Walczak, who also poured over every line with expertise.

To family members and friends who helped me piece our story together by willingly sharing their memories and perspectives.

To our extended family: Peter and Rayan Anaster, David and Lillian Ewert, Gary and Karen Phillips, Ernest and Maxine Ray, and Brad and Barbara Settle who supported our immediate family in a thousand ways.

To our five-star daughters, Jana, Sharon, and Elisabeth, who believed our story should be told. Their memories, comments, editing, encouragement, and computer savvy have been invaluable to me.

And to my dear Barry, for supporting me as, together, we shared our story of trust in God's faithfulness and grace. To Him be all glory and praise.

ENDNOTES

Chapter One

[1] Joe Grata, "Two Turnpike Crashes in Fog Kill 4, Hurt 25," *Post-Gazette*, April 6, 2003, http://www.post-gazette.com/localnews/20030405pike0406p3.asp.

[2] James 4:14, 15, NKJV, italics added.

[3] Lynn Rosellini, "Road Warriors," *Reader's Digest*, September 2003, 28.

[4] Rosellini, 27-30.

[5] 2 Kings 6.

Chapter Two

[1] Hebrews 12:2, italics added.

[2] Psalm 18:30, 32.

[3] 1 Samuel 13:14; Acts 13:22.

[4] Psalm 31:14, 19.

[5] Psalm 138:8, NKJV.

[6] Psalm 138:8.

[7] Philippians 1:6; Hebrews 13:5, 6.

[8] Ken Gire, *The Reflective Life: Becoming More Spiritually Sensitive to the Everyday Moments of Life*, (Colorado Springs: Chariot Victor Publishing, 1998), 57.

[9] Definitions from *The Amplified Bible, Classic Edition (AMPC)*.

[10] James Strong, *Strong's Exhaustive Concordance: Greek Dictionary of the New Testament*, (Tulsa: American Christian College Press), #1411, 24.

[11] Ibid., #5048, 71.

[12] 2 Corinthians 12:9, NKJV.

[13] *The Women's LINK*, Winter 2013, Volume 53, page 2.

[14] http://www.sherryboykin.com/2014/08/down-broadway-without-the-neon-lights-stardom-and-fortune/.

[15] A. W. Tozer, *We Travel an Appointed Way: Making Spiritual Progress*, (Camp Hill: WingSpread Publishers, 2010), 1. Compiled and Edited by Harry Verploegh.

Chapter Three

[1] John 20:25.
[2] John 12:16.
[3] John 20:26-28.
[4] John 3:16.
[5] John 20:29.
[6] 2 Corinthians 5:7.
[7] Frances J. Crosby, "My Savior First of All," 1891, Public Domain.

Chapter Four

[1] Isaiah 14:24, 27.
[2] Isaiah 46:9-11.
[3] Romans 4:21, *The Amplified Bible, Classic Edition (AMPC)*.
[4] Corrie ten Boom, *The Hiding Place*, http://www.whatchristianswanttoknow.com/corrie-ten-boom-quotes-24-favorites/.
[5] Philippians 1:12-14.
[6] Psalm 46:1, *The Amplified Bible*.
[7] 1 Peter 1:6, 7.
[8] Hebrews 12:1-3.

Chapter Five

[1] The medical staff in Altoona informed Jana that her dad was found near a red pickup truck which, according to the police report, caught on fire after the family exited the vehicle. Later, someone else said he was cut out of the back left side of the car.
[2] John 11:21.
[3] John 11:37.
[4] Elizabeth George, *Loving God With All Your Mind*, (Eugene: Harvest House Publishers, 1994), 32, 33.

Chapter Six

[1] Elizabeth Barrett Browning, *Aurora Leigh*, 1857, Public Domain.
[2] 2 Chronicles 16:9.
[3] Proverbs 5:21; 15:3, italics added.
[4] John 11:4, 15.
[5] John 11:40.
[6] John 11:42.
[7] John 11:38, 43, 44.
[8] John 11:45.
[9] The Rancho Los Amigos Scale of Cognitive Functioning is a tool used

to describe a brain-injured patient's level of behavior, from deep coma to appropriate behavior and cognitive functioning. It includes eight stages, from Level I (No Response) to Level VIII (Purposeful and Appropriate). This information is taken from a book given to us by John Heinz Institute of Rehabilitation: *Living With Brain Injury: A Guide for Families* by Richard Senelick, MD, and Karla Dougherty, 2nd ed. (Birmingham: HealthSouth Press, 2001), 56-58.

[10] Ephesians 3:20.

[11] John 11:4.

Chapter Eight

[1] Hebrews 13:21.

[2] James 1: 2, 3, *The Amplified Bible, Classic Edition (AMPC).*

[3] Robert J. Morgan, *The Red Sea Rules: 10 God-given Strategies for Difficult Times*, (Nashville: Thomas Nelson Publishers, 2001), 96.

[4] Romans 5:3, 4.

Chapter Ten

[1] Proverbs 4:23, *The Amplified Bible, Classic Edition (AMPC).*

[2] Matthew 12:34.

[3] Philippians 1:6.

[4] Galatians 4:4, 5.

[5] Jerry Bridges quoting John Brown, *Expository Discourses on 1 Peter* (1848; reprint edition, Edinburgh: The Banner of Truth Trust, Volume 1), 106.

[6] Jerry Bridges, *The Pursuit of Holiness*, (Colorado Springs: NavPress, 1996), 47.

[7] 2 Corinthians 5:21.

Chapter Twelve

[1] Romans 15:4.

[2] 2 Corinthians 1:8-11, italics added.

[3] Jim Elliot and four other missionary men made contact with the Huaorani or Auca Indians in Ecuador, hoping to share the gospel with them. The Indians speared them to death on January 8, 1956. Jim's widow, Elisabeth, along with their small daughter and Rachel Saint, sister of one of the martyrs, managed to go back to these same people, learn their language, and tell them about a God who loved them and sent His Son to be their Savior. The story is told in Elisabeth Elliot's book, *Through Gates of Splendor.*

[4] Elisabeth Elliot, *Secure in the Everlasting Arms*, (Ann Arbor: Servant Publications, 2002), p. 73.

[5] Ibid., p. 37.

[6] Deuteronomy 33:25, KJV.

[7] Elliot, p. 52.
[8] Ibid., pp. 79, 80.

Chapter Thirteen

[1] Luke 12:15.
[2] Colossians 3:2.
[3] Ephesians 3:20.
[4] The Montrose Christian Writers Conference in Montrose, PA.
[5] 2 Corinthians 4:16-18, italics added.

Chapter Fourteen

[1] Psalm 139:14.
[2] 1 Corinthians 12:26.
[3] Job 1:1-5.
[4] Job 2:9.
[5] Job 2:10.
[6] Elliot, p. 183.

Chapter Fifteen

[1] Dorothy A. Thrupp (1779-1847), "Savior, Like a Shepherd Lead Us," 1836, Public Domain.
[2] Annie Johnson Flint (1866-1932), "He Giveth More Grace," Public Domain.

Chapter Sixteen

[1] Meredith Colohan, "Always for the Other Guy," *The Abington Journal*, June 3, 2015, pg. 1A, 4A.
[2] Psalm 18:30-32.
[3] 2 Samuel 7:3.
[4] 1 Kings 8:18, 19.
[5] 2 Samuel 7:22, 28.
[6] Kay Arthur, *As Silver Refined: Learning to Embrace Life's Disappointments,* (Colorado Springs: Waterbrook Press, 1997), 28.
[7] Proverbs 16:9.
[8] Proverbs 19:21.
[9] James 1:12.

Chapter Seventeen

[1] James 3:17, NKJV.
[2] Proverbs 9:4-6, *The Amplified Bible, Classic Edition (AMPC)*.
[3] Proverbs 14:15b, *The Amplified Bible, Classic Edition (AMPC)*.

Chapter Eighteen

[1] Hebrews 4:15.

[2] Hebrews 4:16.

[3] 2 Corinthians 1:3, 4.

[4] 2 Corinthians 1:4, *The Amplified Bible. Classic Edition (AMPC).*

[5] John 5:6.

[6] John 5:8.

[7] 2 Corinthians 2:14, NKJV.

Chapter Nineteen

[1] Psalm 56:3, KJV.

[2] 2 Timothy 1:7, NKJV.

[3] Psalm 139:5.

[4] Grace L. Fabian, *Outrageous Grace: A Story of Tragedy and Forgiveness,* (Bloomington: iUniverse, Inc., 2013), 76.

[5] Genesis 12:1.

[6] 1 Peter 3:4.

[7] 1 Peter 3:6.

[8] 1 Peter 3:6, *The Amplified Bible, Classic Edition (AMPC).*

[9] Romans 8:28, *The Amplified Bible, Classic Edition (AMPC).*

[10] Psalm 23:3.

Chapter Twenty

[1] 2 Timothy 4:7.

[2] Revelation 21:4.

[3] 1 Peter 1:4.

[4] Revelation 22:5.

[5] Revelation 21:27.

[6] Revelation 22:3, 4, parentheses added.

[7] C. S. Lewis, *Mere Christianity*, (New York: Macmillan Publishing Company, 1960). p. 118. Copyright 1943, 1945, 1952 by Macmillan Publishing Company, a division of Macmillan, Inc. Rev. ed. first published in 1952. First paperback edition 1960.

[8] Hebrews 11:13, 16.